WHITE DWARF

ISSUE 473

CLASH OF THE TACTICS TITANS

LYLE LOWERY
Managing Editor

The Battle Report is often cited as one of our readers' favourite regular features, and it is certainly a staple of *White Dwarf*. Heck, we're pioneers of the whole Battle Report concept!

We usually centre our Battle Reports around narrative and storytelling, captured with beautiful photos and immersive text. It's a bit less common that we feature tournament-level matched play games, focusing on tactics and strategy rather than telling a cinematic story. But we know there's an appetite for competitive Battle Reports, so for those readers, this issue is for you.

We invited Lawrence Baker and Stephen Box to the Warhammer Studio to play a tournament-level game using the new War Zone: Nachmund Grand Tournament mission pack. These guys are Warhammer 40,000

playtesters with top tournament credentials, not to mention their popular Warhammer media channels – Tabletop Tactics and Vanguard Tactics respectively.

Lawrence and Stephen played an excellent, tightly contested game of Warhammer 40,000 in tournament conditions, and we took a new approach to the Battle Report to capture as much of the tactical nuance and the tips and wisdom the players offered as we could. This Battle Report is loaded with maps depicting the manoeuvres and attrition (an often-requested feature!), as well as photographs of the action with overlays that illustrate key moments of the battle.

We'd love to hear what you think about this Battle Report and Battle Reports in general! What would you like to see in future Battle Reports? Drop us a line at team@ whitedwarf.co.uk!

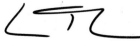

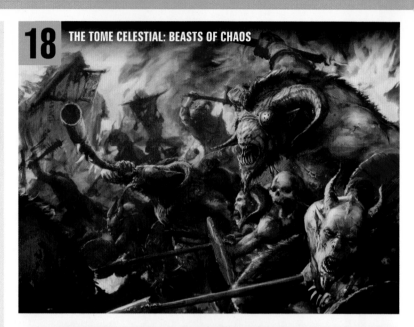

18 THE TOME CELESTIAL: BEASTS OF CHAOS

36 A TALE OF FOUR WARLORDS

62 BATTLE REPORT: DEATH AND ZEAL

82 THE ENEMY WITHIN

124 HONOUR BANNERS

ON THIS ISSUE'S TEAR-OUT SHEET ...

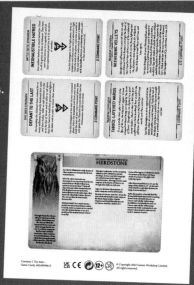

This issue's tear out section includes two useful resources. The first is a set of four Stratagems for Craftworld Altansar. Simply cut them out and keep them with the rest of your Stratagems so you know which ones you want to use in game. The second is a warscroll for the Beasts of Chaos Herdstone, enabling you to utilise the savage power of this terrain piece in your beastly army.

CONTACT

STAR LETTER

INDUSTRIAL GRANDEUR

Hey folk at *White Dwarf*,

I am a long-time Warhammer follower, starting with *White Dwarf* 101, and I wanted to say I appreciate all your efforts with the Warhammer Community and *White Dwarf* articles. Ever since the new Warhammer came around, I have to say I have really enjoyed being part of the community and seeing new and old stuff I have not seen before. It's been a tough year for lots of folk – I personally lost my mother due to Covid-19 complications not so long ago, and one of the constants through it all has been the hobby in some form or another. A few years back, I finally met my long-held idol, John Blanche, through blogging about my hobby, and ever since, I have been a part of a small group of skirmish wargaming enthusiasts.

It has been wonderful seeing all the new and positive changes during this time. I am mixed race and was born in Britain during the seventies, and as such, I was never really represented in my hobby during the early years in eighties and nineties. It's not a thing I would often mention as it can distract from the real reason I game: for fun! But that does not mean that race has never been an issue – it's just one I was happy enough to sideline for my hobby and just get on with it. It has been a real pleasure seeing the tentative steps GW has made towards rectifying this, first with Age of Sigmar and, more recently, with the new Cadian heads. It's a small thing, but if I had the option to have a model represent me when I was a child, I think it would have helped in so many little unspoken ways.

Anyhow, I just wanted to say thank you for all the inspiring and unceasing work you folk do (and everyone else involved in bringing this shared fantasy to life). Oh, by the way, I created a thing last year during lockdown that I am quite proud of. It's a small spire on Necromunda (Belakspur) – a lifelong ambition now realised with the help of all the wonderful new architectural kits available from you guys. I was going to host a huge gaming event, and this was going to be the centerpiece last year, but due to restrictions as well as losing my job, I couldn't run the event. Now it looks like it won't happen at all, which is a shame as I worked on it for over a year … but I thought you guys might appreciate it.

Keep up the inspiring work, folk; it's appreciated.

Neil Reed
Leeds

It's been a very strange year for all of us, and we are glad that Warhammer has helped you to cope with these difficult times.

Your Necromunda board is absolutely amazing! It really captures the sprawling, decaying grandeur and oppressive mood of the hive cities. We can only imagine the amount of time and dedication required to build such an impressive piece of architecture. We're sorry you didn't get to play on it, but who knows what the future holds. Perhaps you will get the chance some day!

EMAIL US:
TEAM@WHITEDWARF.CO.UK

FIND US ON FACEBOOK:
@WARHAMMEROFFICIAL

WRITE TO US:
THE WHITE DWARF BUNKER
GAMES WORKSHOP
NOTTINGHAM
NG7 2WS
UNITED KINGDOM

By submitting letters, articles or photographs, you give Games Workshop permission to feature them in White Dwarf, on the Warhammer Community page or on Facebook at any time in the future. To read our full privacy policy, see the White Dwarf Privacy Notice in the Customer Services section on:

www.games-workshop.com

Space Wolf Primaris Redemptor Dreadnought
by Charles de Bellabre

Iron Hills Dwarves
with Crossbows
by Jakub Bartkowiak

Wurrgog Prophet
by John Wilson

The Wurmspat
by Maciej Sadowski

PAINTING QUESTION: KRAGNOS

Hey there, Grombrindal – I'm hoping you can answer a question that has been bugging me. I just bought the great Kragnos model, and, while I'm painting the furs in different colours, I want to paint his shield and jewellery in the box-art style. I'm wondering how this was done, since they look kind of metallic but not.

**Dan Deakin
Oxford, UK**

We can definitely help you, Dan. Here's what 'Eavy Metal's Max Faleij has to say about painting Kragnos.

Max: The main shield is actually not painted with many metallics at all. It's basecoated with Sons of Horus Green, then shaded with a mix of Sons of Horus Green, Naggaroth Night and Abaddon Black. It's highlighted with a mix of Sons of Horus Green and Deepkin Flesh, then glazed with thin layers of Akhelian Green, Skeleton Horde and Rhinox Hide to build up the weathering. Some of the details were then picked out in Runelord Brass and Liberator Gold before being glazed back with a mix of Sotek Green, Sons of Horus Green and Nuln Oil. The final highlights involved mixing Deepkin Flesh into the metallics in some places and Stormhost Silver in others to create variety.

The trinkets and chains and other details were painted in a similar way, but some of them start at the metallic stage to create different looks and textures. Some also miss out the Naggaroth Night, again to add variety.

METAL

Basecoat: Sons of Horus Green	Glaze: Akhelian Green, Skeleton Horde & Rhinox Hide 1:1:1
Shade: Sons of Horus Green, Naggaroth Night & Abaddon Black 1:1:1	Detailing: Runelord Brass & Liberator Gold
Highlight: Sons of Horus Green & Deepkin Flesh 1:1	Glaze: Sotek Green, Sons of Horus Green & Nuln Oil
	Highlight: Deepkin Flesh

Shadow Warriors by Stephan Löppmann

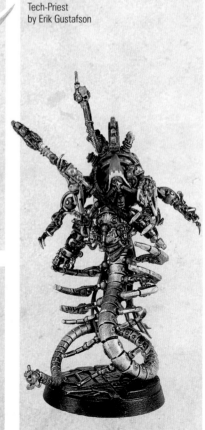

Tech-Priest by Erik Gustafson

Pippin, Merry, Sam and Frodo by Kev Lawrence

T'au diorama display
by Phil Larrassey

ASK GROMBRINDAL

Greetings, Mighty Short One. Orks from the Snakebite Clan prefer 'da old ways', so are they against travel via space hulk? If so, how do they travel between planets?

Rufus O'Malley
Sydney, Australia

Mighty Short One? Is that a compliment or an insult? Thinking about it, it's probably just a fact! In answer to your question, Snakebites do travel on space hulks. Space hulks can't really be controlled, so there's no fiddly technology to deal with, and Orks have been using space hulks for thousands of years, if not more, so to lots of Snakebites, travelling in this way probably counts as 'da old ways'. Even hitching a ride on a kroozer probably doesn't count. Being grizzled pragmatists, they might make deals with other Ork Clans to transport them from world to world, complaining all the way about the unnaturalness of it all. Then again, some of them might see their spacecraft as some huge void-beast, happily snagging it and riding the dangerous 'creature' to the next good punch-up. Orks are rarely philosophically consistent!

Grombrindal

A TIME FOR ILLUMINATION

Dear Games Workshop. Please find attached a copy of a letter written by my son, Jacobi Short, age seven. Also attached is a coloured picture by him and Space Marine Chapter models of his own design that he helped his dad to paint. His letter reads:

'To Games Workshop, I am making up a new Space Marine army called the Illuminators, and their worst enemy is the Death Guard. They are blue and yellow. Their Chapter Master is called Jacobi.'

I hope you enjoy this, he's a huge fan of the Warhammer 40,000 universe.

Sophie and Jacobi Short
Andover, UK

Now this is some excellent creativity, Jacobi! You've designed an awesome colour scheme for your Space Marines, given them an exciting and inspirational name (we could all do with some extra illumination these days!) and then you and your dad have painted some impressive models ready for battle. Perfect! We look forward to hearing what they get up to on the battlefield! For anyone else wanting to create their own Space Marine Chapter, you can find the outline Jacobi used on the Warhammer Community site. Simply search for the 'Space Marine Heraldry' download.

TOP PHOTO TIPS

In Contact, we want to show off the very best miniatures painted by you, our readers. Of course, great miniatures need great pictures, so we came up with a useful guide to help you out:

www.warhammer-community.com/the-model-photo

If you follow all the advice in that article, you really can't go far wrong. Our top tips are:

Always use a white background.

Make sure you've got good lighting.

Ensure the whole model is in focus, including the base and all its weapons.

Find the model's golden angle. If in doubt, take a look at the same model on the Games Workshop website to see how it was photographed.

MODEL OF THE MONTH: SMAUG

Our model of the month is this stunning rendition of Smaug from *The Hobbit* movie trilogy, painted by Daniel Brescia. We asked him how he painted the iconic dragon.

Daniel: I started by spraying Smaug Mephiston Red, then airbrushing a mix of Mephiston Red, Khorne Red and Naggaroth Night into the recessed areas. Next I applied a wash of Carroburg Crimson to the whole model. The tips of the wings and throat were airbrushed with Mephiston Red mixed with Jokaero Orange, followed by Troll Slayer Orange and finally Fire Dragon Bright. His scales are painted with a mix of Khorne Red, Naggaroth Night and Abaddon Black and then highlighted with Fulgrim Pink. His underbelly is painted Zandri Dust, washed Reikland Fleshshade and then highlighted with Karak Stone, Ushabti Bone and Screaming Skull.

WARHAMMER AGE OF SIGMAR

From the maelstrom of a sundered world, the Eight Realms were born. And with their birth began a war to claim them. This issue: four huge armies, war in Beastbridge and new rules for Warcry.

TOME CELESTIAL
The Tome Celestial goes beast mode on page 18. A battletome update for the Beasts of Chaos follows, as well as a campaign arc to theme your games!

A TALE OF FOUR WARLORDS
Martyn, Miyuki, Rich and Calum have finally made it to the end of their epic challenge. Turn to page 36 to see their incredible armies in all their glory!

THE BRIGHT CITY

The city of Hammerhal numbers amongst the greatest achievements of Sigmar's folk. Outside Azyr, no stronghold of the God-King is greater than this one. Or, more accurately, these two, for Hammerhal is so vast that it extends into both Aqshy and Ghyran.

ASH HAND BURROWS

PILLARS OF INFINITY

CHARCOAL HILL

CINDERWORM

PERSPICARIUM

CANDLE TOWN

PYROMANCER'S TOR

SCORCHED BONE MARSHES

ASHBARK TOWER

BRIARGATE WOOD

BLOOM GATE TERRACE

THE NARROWS

BRIAR BRIDGE

STORMRIFT REALMGATE

DEEP GATE FIELDS

THE CAULDRON

ONYX SHORE

GREAT CATHEDRAL OF SIGMAR

RAVEN BRIDGE

HEART OF RUBEUS

BONES OF KAZARIG

GOLDENPATH

THORN GATE THICKET

THE BRASS MIRE

JADEHEART GLADES

STORMFALL

THE CLEAVE

WILLOW GATE WOODS

FOREST OF THE VINE GATE

LAVAFALL DISTRICT

KINDLE HEIGHTS

THE FYRE POTS

HALLS OF SHAPING

BLACK DUST ALLEYS

THE BLACKGLASS GUILDS

CRYSTALARIUM

THE RHUIN PEAK

F ittingly for a settlement established in the volatile heartlands of Aqshy, Hammerhal Aqsha was born amidst a storm of blood. Its foundations were being laid even as Sigmar's chosen warriors battled against the seemingly endless tides of savage orruks who dwelt in the core regions of the Great Parch. Since the first hours of its existence, Hammerhal Aqsha has teetered on the precipice of extinction. It is testament to the grit of its inhabitants that the city has expanded to become arguably the greatest glory of Sigmar's empire.

Hammerhal is known as the Twin-Tailed City. It has expanded to spill across both the Aqshian and Ghyranite sides of the Stormrift Realmgate, each half supporting the other with vital supplies that would be otherwise difficult to acquire in their home realm. That being said, the residents of Hammerhal Aqsha have long considered it to be the city's premier half. It is in Aqsha that Hammerhal's Grand Conclave maintains its council chambers – the Stormrift Palace – and Aqshy's warlike people have provided formidable manpower for Sigmar's campaigns. Many Aqshian citizens feel a sense of superiority to the 'greenfingers' of their sister city. However, the Ghyranites are quick to take umbrage with this notion, pointing out how they maintain a steady supply of food even as their own home comes under constant attack. Brawls erupt almost nightly as these prejudices find violent release.

Over the century or so since its founding, Hammerhal Aqsha has expanded rapidly. The Perspicarium, Stormkeep of the Hammers of Sigmar, continues to watch over the city from atop the hollow obsidian shelf known as the Basalarach – mightiest of the so-called Pillars of Infinity. Surrounding it is the gilded Old Town of Aqsha, where the city's rich and powerful reside. For a teeming megalopolis often blighted by ash storms and acid rains, Hammerhal Aqsha still has its enclaves of relative beauty, most prominent of which are the Great Cathedral of Sigmar and the forested Greenward Prefecture, where Sylvaneth ambassadors reside.

Yet, for the majority of Aqsha's inhabitants, such grandeur is a distant dream. They are instead consigned to inhabit the slum regions known as the Drudges – districts such as Cinderfall, which have been overwhelmed by the city's rate of expansion and collapsed into barely policed hives of vice and inequity – or even to live amongst the frontier 'bulwark' communities that lie outside the walls. Food can be difficult to come by, and many of these impoverished souls earn a livelihood in the sweltering industrial zones of the city, producing arms and prefabricated structures for its Dawnbringer ventures. Small wonder that so many citizens later choose to join these crusading armies, betting everything on the dubious promise of a new life amidst the wilds.

THE GNARLED GATE WOOD

SOOT CLOUD GARDENS

FYRE FISH MARKETS

TALLOW PARK

BLACKWOOD TOWN

FOREST OF THE OAKEN GATE

STORMHORN MOUNT

FOREST OF THE BRACKEN GATE

HEARTFIRE PROMONTORY

THE COGWORKS

RUNE KEY TOWER

TO FORGE A BLAZING PATH

The Dawnbringer Crusades that march forth from Hammerhal Aqsha are the grandest of any free city. Few settlements can match the industrial potential or sheer reserves of manpower that Hammerhal can muster – to say nothing of the potency and diversity of the warriors who make up its armies and their burning drive to succeed.

As far as the logisticians who take on the endless task of cataloguing Sigmar's wars can verify, Hammerhal Aqsha has been the source of more Dawnbringer Crusades than any other stronghold of the God-King. Some of these, such as the Third Aridian Venture or the Caustic Ranging, were truly grand undertakings. Countless others were far more modest, doomed to ignoble ends in the hostile lands of Aqshy. Yet no matter how many crusades falter, no matter how many settlers meet a grisly demise, Hammerhal Aqsha continues to churn out new expeditions. The city has become a furnace that tempers armies rather than clay, and much of its production capacity is now given over to forging the manifold weapons and transportable domiciles that aspiring crusaders need to found new strongpoints.

Military service and pride has become a defining trait of Hammerhal Aqsha's citizenry. Even the lowliest inhabitant of the Drudges can name several great victories won by the city's armies, and thousands gather each third week of Azyr's Gleaming to watch the sacred battle standards of Hammerhal be paraded through the streets. The Stormcasts of the Hammers of Sigmar, golden guardians of the city, are revered as warrior-saints. When they walk the

streets, citizens throng around them in chanting mobs, fighting one another for a chance to lay hands upon the Stormcasts' holy trappings. For many inhabitants of the Twin-Tailed City, service in the 'Goldjackets' – a general name applied to all Hammerhal Aqsha's Freeguilds, though each regiment has its own unique moniker and speciality, such as the artillerists of the Leaden Bulls or the elite Vandusian Guard – is the easiest way out of their harsh existences. To accept the Coin Malleus and join a Dawnbringer Crusade is the prevailing dream of many of the city's youth.

While Hammerhal Aqsha has its share of pampered highborn wastrels, many of Sigmar's new nobility have earned their accolades on the battlefield and have the scars to prove it. It is tradition amongst several aristocratic lineages for all children – whether born in wedlock or scandal, for Hammerhal has no room for

wasted potential – to receive at least some measure of schooling in the famed Acadamae Martial. Through this practice, should the worst ever come to pass and its walls be breached, Hammerhal would not be lacking for capable militia commanders. The Dragoon Generals of Hammerhal are particularly masterful cavalry commanders, whose famed mounted echelons have turned the tide in many battles.

While the inherent Hammerhalian spirit goes a fair way to explain the regularity with which it musters new Dawnbringer Crusades, propaganda is another tool used by the city's leaders to feed their conquests. This is the domain of the Church Unberogen, for it is the priests and Arch Lectors who fund many of the printing houses of Hammerhal, which in turn distribute motivational scroll-scraps amongst the populace that encourage them to take up arms and seek their fortune.

The church has long mastered the art of condensing stirring rhetoric to a series of short and effective maxims delivered at just the right moment to tip a wavering soul over into pure zealotry. Many of these mantras have been taken up by the 'Dawners', converted into stirring battle-cries and marching songs that are eagerly encouraged by the priesthood. The presence of the Great Cathedral of Sigmar gives the Church Unberogen a near-unrivalled pulpit from which to disseminate its message, and its lay preachers are a common sight, even in the most dilapidated nooks of the city, tending to petty shrines and filling the heads of any who will listen with Sigmar's conquering ideals.

While the majority of Hammerhal Aqsha's population is drawn from humble human stock, they are far from the only beings to join the city's armies in the Dawnbringer Crusades. Aqsha has a sizable duardin population that has been essential to the expansion of the city and its industrial capacity. Throngs and clans of these doughty warriors accompany most Hammerhalian Dawnbringer Crusades, for their expertise is invaluable when it comes to establishing resolute strongholds under great pressure and to an unrelenting schedule. The wider duardin race also has a regular presence alongside the city's army in the form of the Fyreslayers, whose mercenary fyrds are often hired by the leaders of Hammerhal to join its armies.

Various aelven communities also number amongst Aqsha's populace. Though the recent annexation of Anvilgard in the north of the Great Parch has stirred up tension with these subcultures, particularly the bloodthirsty Daughters of Khaine, few Hammerhalians would reject their worthy blades on the day of battle. Much of the population holds a grudging respect for the aggression and warrior skill of Morathi's disciples. Alongside these line forces come the more esoteric elements of Aqsha's armies: pyromancers, who travel in great floating towers; battle preachers, who proselyte from war altars dragged by numberless fanatics; and, of course, the Hammers of Sigmar, who fearlessly hurl themselves into every foe who dares stand against them.

'Hammerhal has, in the past, been likened to a powder keg, needing but one errant spark to detonate spectacularly. Of course, we have errant sparks, cinders and flames aplenty here in Aqshy, so the comparison perhaps lacks some nuance. I instead prefer to think of our noble city as akin to the volcanoes claimed by Grimnir's folk; maybe one day we will blow ourselves apart in a storm of sound and fury, but God-King preserve you if you're in our vicinity when we do.'

– Sevastian Mensch, Master Patriarch of Hammerhal Aqsha

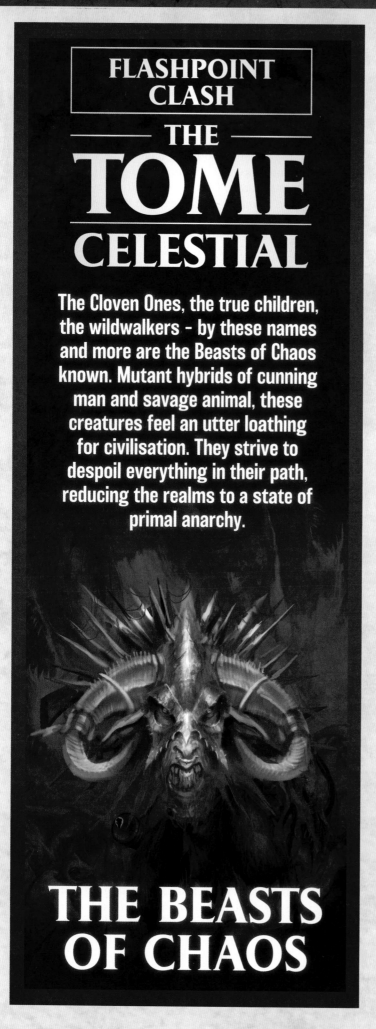

THE TOME CELESTIAL

THE BEASTS OF CHAOS

The Cloven Ones, the true children, the wildwalkers – by these names and more are the Beasts of Chaos known. Mutant hybrids of cunning man and savage animal, these creatures feel an utter loathing for civilisation. They strive to despoil everything in their path, reducing the realms to a state of primal anarchy.

Across the realms, grim fables warn the unwary not to stray into the warped wilderness. In these places – at the heart of malevolent forests and in the depths of rock-mawed canyons – horned figures dwell, twisted by dark powers and filled with bottomless hatred. These beasts who walk as men are predators in the truest sense, able to stalk unseen until a deafening horn-blast signals their prey's doom. When their armies spill forth, it is to topple the walls of civilisation and tear apart any who would defend them. Waves of Chaotic energy accompany their warpath, bringing grotesque mutation and madness. These creatures are the beastmen, mortal embodiments of ruin.

Beastmen come in many forms, but the most numerous are those known as the gor-kin. Gors are typically humanoid in appearance, though they possess twisted bestial features and a more savage mien. They walk upon cloven hooves, their muscular bodies are marked by patches of coarse fur, and their brows are often crested with protruding horns. Horns are of great importance in beastman society as a symbol of might. While the lowly ungors will sport little more than nubs of bone sprouting from their temples, the Beastlord chieftains are blessed with huge, imposing antlered crowns. Not all beastmen have bovine or goat-like features; some possess snapping shark-maws, the lithe upper bodies of hunting cats or crooked avian beaks. All, however, will respect a champion endowed with majestic horns and need little excuse to follow them to war.

To a beastman, strength is everything. Their culture is crude but robust, with the mightiest creatures brutally imposing their will on their lesser ilk. When they strike out in force against their many despised adversaries, they are joined by all manner of Chaos-touched monsters. Bullgors – hulking tauroids cursed by an endless hunger for blood – charge out from their lairs howling crazed, wordless battle-cries. With them come horrors such as slavering mutant wolfhounds, shrieking Cockatrices and the sanity-blasting aberrations known as Jabberslythes, to name but a few. Most powerful of all the gor-kin's allies are the Dragon Ogors of the Thunderscorn beastherds. This race of scaly, centauroid immortals was cast out from its domains long ago by rival powers and forced to skulk in the forgotten places. They now seek vengeance with a hateful passion, wielding the might of dark storms to blast their foes to ashes.

As a beastherd advances, the energy of Chaos gathers around it. This is the stuff of corruption in its rawest state, revered by the gor-kin and attracted by their deep-seated malice. This unclean force is wielded by the Bray-Shamans in displays of savage sorcery, and it quickly sinks deep into the land itself. Here it will break down the laws of creation, forming nexuses of tortured earth upon which are erected horned monoliths known as Herdstones. Around these lodestones, the beastmen make their camps and perform sacrifices to the old darkness. In the Era of the Beast, the gor-kin have been bolstered by the bestial power of Ghur as it crashes across the cosmos. They see it as their holy duty to meld this animalistic magic with the dark essence of Chaos, just as they themselves are a melding of man and beast. It is their desire to see this corrupting hybrid magic wash over all lands, reducing everything to a primordial nightmare in which the beastmen alone would be the apex predators.

MASTERS OF THE WARPED WILDS

Before the man-god Sigmar ever walked the realms and brought civilisation to their native peoples, the Cloven Ones dwelled in their ancient lands. The shamans of the beastmen are the keepers of their oral traditions, but even they have no singular answer for how the first gor-kin came into being. Some say that all beastmen descend from a single primogenitor – the legendary Gorfather, the first creature in all the Mortal Realms to heed the powers of Chaos. Others believe that the energies of ruin leaked into the realmspheres long ago, and where they pooled, animals were granted the gift of mutation. In the case of the Dragon Ogors, legend states that their ancestors made a pact with the Chaos Gods in the first days of the World-that-Was, receiving immortality in exchange for eternal servitude. That ill-considered oath binds them to this day, granting the arrogant beasts no rest even in the Mortal Realms.

This atavistic pedigree goes some way to explaining the beastmen's profound loathing of civilisation and all its works. In the depths of their subconscious, every gor recognises that there was a time when they were the masters of the wildlands. The races that now claim widespread dominion were nothing more than hapless prey to be hunted and slaughtered at leisure. It was only the coming of the Pantheon of Order and the unity they brought to many tribal peoples that saw the beastmen forced out of their ancestral territories and into the inhospitable wildernesses, places where only they could

hope to survive. The seething hatred born from this reversal fuels the gor-kin's need to cast down and despoil, so the old ways might come again.

One might expect the beastmen to feel some kinship with the barbarous children of Gorkamorka, but this is not the case. Those creatures that venerate the twin-headed god have no love for civilisation, but each – whether they realise it or not – seeks to reshape the realms into a state that suits their kind. There is nothing natural about the beastmen's designs. They would trample the lands into a ruin that could then be suffused with the raw energies of Chaos and, in the most extreme cases, would see reality itself crumble. The gor-kin perhaps do not loathe the greenskins with the same intensity they do men, aelves and duardin, recognising in them equally savage souls who understand that only raw strength grants the right to rule. Only rarely, however, do encounters between the two races not end in horrific bloodshed.

Though they revel in their nature as creatures of primal Chaos, most beastmen have little interest in the Great Game of the Dark Gods. They often show contempt for daemons, seeing them as puppets leashed to a greater entity, and rarely beseech the Brothers in Darkness directly; power is to be taken, not asked for. Even so, the beastmen respect the Chaos Gods as primordial forces of corruption. Looted trophies and sacrificed corpses are left to them around the Herdstones, and most gor-kin will fight alongside the servants of the gods should their aims align. In turn, the Ruinous Powers derive great amusement from the rampages of the Cloven Ones, delighting in the disaster they bring to the servants of rival deities.

With all this said, it is not unheard of for some beastmen to be lured in by the whispers of one god or another. Their mind's eye flickers with the promise of power beyond any they have ever known or a chance to vent their hatred of mortalkind that much more effectively. When such a bargain is struck, the gods are not miserly in blessing their malformed offspring, twisting their bodies further to resemble the whims of their patron and filling their souls with unholy purpose. Entire herds have been known to swear themselves to a god in this fashion, forming warbands of Khorngors, Pestigors, Tzaangors or Slaangors.

However, while the gor-kin will follow these ascended creatures if they display suitable strength, many recognise the trap within this bargain. By tethering their souls to a higher power, the devoted creature becomes nothing more than a pawn, one that can be discarded at a moment's notice. Many chieftains and shamans teach that it is more worthy to rely on one's own might and to offer worship to the power of ruin in its most primordial state than to be lured into the service of a single aspect of Chaos. Ironically, this often leaves the feral gor-kin the wiser party when compared to blinkered mortals who believe they can receive the boons of the Dark Gods without ever paying a price. To the humble folk of the realms who find themselves on the killing end of a beastmen stampede, however, such nuances of opinion do nothing to save them from a grisly fate.

THE SHADOWGAVE

In the same way that they offer wary respect to the powers of Chaos, the beastmen honour all manner of atavistic spirits and mutant godbeasts. Many Greatfray tribes are influenced by the history and mythology of their own hunting grounds, but there is one entity that has slunk into the minds of all gor-kin. Even the weakest ungor can recognise this entity by its manifold names – the Shadowgave, the Beast that Devours, the Bringer of Devolution. The Shadowgave is an entity said to be older than thought and time, a spirit of primal malignancy that feasts upon strife. In the World-that-Was, it manifested in the form of Morghur, a gor whose body was constantly in flux and who poisoned the enchanted forests of that world with his very presence. Morghur was struck down many times, but always did his immortal spirit recover and incarnate again, for so long as reality inexorably moves towards entropy and dissolution, his essence will endure.

None have seen Morghur since the breaking of the World-that-Was, though in the depths of withered Ghyran, it is said that wanderers may hear strange trilling cries echoing around copses of tormented trees and that the sound is an invitation to madness. Yet the Shadowgave's spirit is believed to live on as whispers in the minds of his bestial children. The Greatfray known as the Gavespawn are his most fervent disciples, and they furiously strive to see the realms collapse into the hellish nothingness that the Shadowgave desires. Many Bray-Shamans have also joined his strange cult, advancing their master's insane agenda with or without the knowledge of their tribal chieftains.

THE TIME OF THE BEAST

Few creatures greeted the dawning of the Era of the Beast with the same glee as the gor-kin. Across the realms, the surge of animalistic energy generated by Ghur was seen as a vindication of their long-held beliefs that the prospering of civilisation had only ever been an anomaly and that a new age was descending to correct the course of history.

The gor-kin's hatred and lust for bloodshed have become so maddening that many are rendered blind to all other concerns. Sigmarite outposts that might have had to endure one or two beastman raids a season are now faced with twice that many or more. The beastmen were always known for their barbarity, but now many seem to have gone truly, violently insane. Like rabid animals, they froth and bellow, trampling swathes of the realms into oblivion.

The Greatfrays hurl themselves forwards in such numbers that their hooves irreparably scar the earth, and the shivering forests belch forth an almost endless stream of snarling abominations. It is the Dawnbringer Crusades against whom the gor-kin display the greatest wrath. To the beastmen, these expeditionary forces represent an unforgivable blasphemy by the forces of civilisation, who now seek not only to strengthen their roots in stolen lands but to expand further into the wilds and raise more of their hateful cities. Worse still, they would purify regions already claimed by blessed corruption, making a mockery of all the beastmen have striven to preserve out in their hunting grounds.

But the gor-kin's skill as ambushers is not to be underestimated. Their warbands trail Dawnbringer Crusades for miles on end, stalking them along secret wild paths and influencing their passage with a subtlety few would expect from beastmen. When the mortals are lost, isolated and at their most vulnerable, the warhorns are sounded, and packs of beastkin emerge to slaughter the

panicked crusaders. It has become a matter of pride amongst rival beastherds to boast of how many crusading hosts they have massacred and to offer up blood-stained trophies of these victories before the Herdstones.

It is when the Dawnbringers reach their destinations and lay down the foundations of new settlements, however, that the fury of the beastmen is truly raised. While the mortals seek to draw upon geomantic energy to power the arcane structures of their new strongpoints, the Bray-Shamans of the gor-kin and Shaggoths of the Thunderscorn have much experience in defiling these natural energies. Through their wild sorcery, ley lines are corrupted and mystical barriers smashed down, allowing throngs of beastmen to overwhelm the settlement. If a geomantic nexus is suitably corrupted, Bray-Shamans have been able to summon vast, fully formed Herdstones through dark sorcery alone, the rock pulsing and groaning as if alive. Around these monoliths, the air boils with the energies of discord, and the revels of the beastmen grow ever more orgiastic and barbaric.

It is not only Dawnbringers who have drawn the ire of the beastmen. During the course of the Soul Wars, many gor-kin became engaged in protracted battles against the dead – contests in which they were determined to prove the victors. Then there are the mortal champions of Chaos. Many of these warriors have long scorned the beastmen, seeing them as nothing more than mindless animals fit only to catch the arrows of their enemies – yet their own presumed favour with the Ruinous Powers has not saved them from being dragged screaming to the gor-kin's altars and sacrificed in hideous rituals that see chieftains of the Cloven Ones swell with divine favour.

If these physical conflicts were the only threat posed by the beastmen, then they would be terrible enough. Yet

'We warned Young Hof many times not to listen too closely to the peddler's tales. But would the lad listen? Nay. He was a Dawner, as he was so fond of saying: a warrior who had marched out from Hammerhal and brought the God-King's light to the tainted lands. What could stories of old shadows in the woods do to unman him?

Perhaps it was our fault. Many dishevelled souls march out on the crusades, risking everything for the chance of a new life. When we saw the peddler shuffling around the streets of New Brighthaven, who would question him? We were so concerned with day-to-day survival that we never thought how strange it was that he wore such heavy cloaks, despite how Aqshy's air always burns, or how his voice carried such a growl. None paid him any attention. If his stories of the Horned Men kept Hof out of trouble, then it was all for the good.

But then, Hof began to change. He started brawling more, first flying off the handle at the slightest provocation then starting fights himself. He began to eat less like a man, tearing into food like a rabid snarlfang. Lumps formed on his forehead, little nubs of bone that the physicians couldn't explain. We heard strange noises coming from his domicile each eve, screams that sounded more like bleats if you listened long enough. One night I found him sniffing ~ literally sniffing ~ around one of the guardian idols, muttering some rhyme I didn't know but that hurt my ears.

Eventually, we could take it no more. Hof's screams were too wild, too animalistic. Everyone snapped. They snatched up torches and pitchforks and marched on his home, intending to burn it to the ground and drag him into the street to ... I shudder to think. They accomplished the former. The latter failed in all the confusion; he got away, making for the edge of the settlement and the kindle-woods beyond. I caught a glance of him in the dim, red light ~ hunched and stooped he was, with one crooked horn sprouting from his brow, braying as he ran on misshapen hooves. When some of us later remembered the peddler and sought him out, he too was gone.

We've seen mutants before, of course. The realms are a mess. But it's worse than that. Hof was a braggart, and he recounted the peddler's stories to the lasses who trailed around after him. We've kept them isolated in their homes for days now, but we can all hear their mewling croaks and brays every night. Then there's what old Magister Larne says about what he sees when he peers into his scrying pool. There's things out there in the forest, evil and twisted things, and they're coming closer. We've sent for reinforcements, but the creatures are approaching too fast. It's almost as if they're being led here ...'

alongside these creeps a subtler, more sinister danger. Outbreaks of mutation, lycanthropy and devolution into animal forms have become increasingly common in the Era of the Beast. The beastmen, however, seem to have discovered some means of weaponising this wave of transformation and turning it to their own twisted ends. In darkest Ghyran, there is a place known as Witherdwell. The power of mutation is said to lie heavy on the air there, and it has long been shunned by the realm's defenders and sealed with great waystones. Since the beginning of the Era of the Beast, Cygors have been sighted around Witherdwell in great numbers, toppling these sacred stones and allowing something terrible to spill forth – the Turnskin Curse.

The Turnskin Curse is no physical sickness; it is a supernatural ailment that spreads like a virus of the mind. To even hear tell of the gor-kin is to risk falling prey to it and to find yourself slowly mutated into one of their kind. Unfortunately, this knowledge is easily passed on in fishwives' tales and tavern gossip, for in many parts of Sigmar's empire, the beastmen are seen only as a myth – the shadow cast by man's primal fear of the woods. In trying to prove their bravery and repeating these stories, the God-King's worshippers have provided the plague with much fertile ground.

Those who succumb to the change and are forced to flee into the wilds are soon picked up by the marauding Greatfrays. At one time, these once-human creatures were referred to contemptuously as 'gaves' and 'turnskins' by the trueborn gors and shown little more respect than the stooped ungors. Yet so many now flood into the camps of the beastmen that it was inevitable that some would rise to become infamous shamans or chieftains. Even those who are weak have their uses, if they can pass for human. These mutants are sent to infiltrate the cities and outposts of Sigmar, concealing their misshapen forms in thick rags and spreading bitter tales of the Cloven Ones to any who will listen and, in doing so, granting the plague a further chance to spread.

It is not only humanity that has received the twin influence of the beastmen and Ghur. In this age of upheaval, animals of all kinds have been touched by an atavistic malice, the darkest aspects of Ghurish magic settling in their souls alongside the sinister touch of Chaos. Stories abound of trusted steeds throwing riders to the ground or otherwise violently lashing out. More sinisterly, in far-flung Sigmarite outposts, there are rumours of livestock cursed by the gor-kin that give birth to hideously deformed hybrid-creatures or even whisper to those sleeping nearby, urging them to slaughter their fellow settlers in outbreaks of deranged violence.

But the beastmen are not the only creatures to have benefited from this new era. There are other powers in tune with the disturbed natural world who might attempt to thwart the ascension of the gor-kin. Of all these foes, none are more despised than the Sylvaneth. The beastmen and the Sylvaneth share an enmity that stretches back to the World-that-Was. They are as opposed in soul as it is

possible to be, for where the forest spirits strive to preserve the cycle of nature, the gor-kin would shatter it completely. Terrible wars have been waged between them to determine the fate of the wildlands, conflicts that have seen entire herds wiped out or Sylvaneth corpses stacked high like so much broken kindling.

For centuries, the beastmen had been gaining the upper hand in these conflicts, but, in recent times, Alarielle the Everqueen – mother-goddess of the Sylvaneth race – has counter-attacked ferociously. Alarielle has cast a mighty Rite of Life, sending the energies of clean rebirth cascading across the realms. Everywhere, trees and fungus grow taller, animals multiply, and the seas heave with coral growths. The power of the Rite manifests as a strident melody that is carried by wargroves of vengeful forest spirits. To the inherently corrupt beastmen, even a note of this song is enough to induce hideous agony – one they will do anything to silence.

Across the Realm of Life, vast armies of monsters have emerged, throwing themselves against places of power sacred to the Sylvaneth. Even as the Rite's tune heals the realm, the forest spirits can hear a constant howling on the edge of perception. This is the soul of the beastman race, pressing ever closer as the Rite's energies are stretched thinner. In places where even the Sylvaneth cannot withstand their fury, the beastmen lead bloodthirsty rituals to corrupt wellsprings of life magic – and with the ley lines transmitting arcane power more rigorously than ever, these ruinous energies can spread far indeed.

Other forces have also drawn strength from the Era of the Beast, and their rise has not gone unnoticed by the beastmen. The hordes of Destruction in particular have become more powerful than ever, especially when led by the returned god Kragnos. So potent is Kragnos' aura of bestial might that even the creatures of Chaos feel energised by his savage, spiritual resonance, however unwillingly. Kragnos, for his part, scorns the beastmen as he scorns all others, and he relishes any opportunity to trample them into oblivion.

However, the Thunderscorn Shaggoths – ancient enemies of Kragnos' lost Drogrukh people – see the End of Empires for what he is. Kragnos is the last of his kind, overcome by grief and rage, and his claims of divinity are as nothing when compared to the true, elemental powers of Chaos. These malevolent creatures have long harboured a desire for vengeance against the Drogrukh as well as the now-returned Draconith; in the wilds of the realms, the summits of lonely peaks are now perpetually swathed in dark, furious stormclouds as the ancient Thunderscorn beastherds make ready to begin a primeval war anew.

> *'Realms awaken. I hear them. Even after Everqueen tried to break me, I hear them. Things stir in their souls. Things with mind and will and hate. Much hate. I seek path to Ghur, where awakening will come first. I seek soul of realm. I will teach it to hate even stronger.'*
>
> **– Ghorraghan Khai, master of the Butcher-herd**

A battletome update contains official new rules that are considered to be part of the battletome that is being updated. Treat them exactly as you would the rules that appear in the battletome itself.

BATTLETOME: BEASTS OF CHAOS UPDATE

Welcome to the *Battletome: Beasts of Chaos* update. Over the following pages, you will find a host of new and exciting rules to use alongside *Battletome: Beasts of Chaos* in open, narrative and matched play.

BATTLE TRAIT

This section of this article a new battle trait, 'The Creatures of Chaos', which includes a table of monstrous rampages that can be carried out by **BEASTS OF CHAOS MONSTERS**.

WARSCROLL UPDATE

This section contains a new warscroll for the Beasts of Chaos Herdstone faction terrain feature.

◉ OPEN PLAY ◉

This section includes twists and ruses that can only be used by a Beasts of Chaos army.

◉ MATCHED PLAY ◉

This section includes grand strategies and battle tactics that can only be used by a Beasts of Chaos army.

◉ PATH TO GLORY ◉

This section contains rules for using your Beasts of Chaos collection in a Path to Glory campaign.

TO HUNT THE DAWN

The last section is a campaign arc for your Beasts of Chaos to play through. It tells a story set on Beastbridge, a land bridge that stretches west of the Great Parch in Aqshy. A Dawnbringer Crusade has come to the region, set on sundering the many Herdstones that have been raised here. The Beasts of Chaos must stop them at all costs.

BATTLE TRAITS

Add the following battle trait to the Battle Traits section in *Battletome: Beasts of Chaos*.

THE CREATURES OF CHAOS

From the untamed regions of the Mortal Realms spill forth hideous monstrosities born from the touch of Chaos. These titanic aberrations are nightmarish to behold, and they follow the call of the Greatfrays to war so they might feast upon the remains of the fallen.

When you carry out a monstrous rampage (core rules, 21.1) with a **BEASTS OF CHAOS MONSTER**, you can carry out 1 of the monstrous rampages that follow instead of any other monstrous rampage you can carry out with that **MONSTER**.

BEASTS OF CHAOS MONSTROUS RAMPAGES

	Primal Roar: Roll a dice. On a 1, nothing happens. On a 2-5, you receive 1 primordial call point. On a 6, you receive 3 primordial call points.
	Feast on Flesh: Only a GHORGON can be picked to carry out this monstrous rampage, and the same unit can only carry out this monstrous rampage once per battle. Improve the Rend characteristic of this model's melee weapons by 1 until the end of the following combat phase. In addition, until the end of the following combat phase, each time an enemy model is slain by an attack made by this model, this model heals a number of wounds equal to the Wounds characteristic of that slain model.
	Devour Spell: Only a CYGOR can be picked to carry out this monstrous rampage. Pick 1 endless spell within 6" of this model and roll 2D6. If the roll exceeds the casting value of the spell that summoned that endless spell, that endless spell is dispelled and this model heals a number of wounds equal to the 2D6 roll.
	Entropic Miasma: Only a JABBERSLYTHE can be picked to carry out this monstrous rampage. Pick 1 enemy HERO within 3" of this model and roll a dice. On a 1, nothing happens. On a 2-5, worsen the Save characteristic of that HERO by 1 (to a minimum of 6+) until the end of the following combat phase. On a 6, worsen the Save characteristic of that HERO by 2 (to a minimum of 6+) until the end of the following combat phase.
	Thricefold Savagery: Only a CHIMERA can be picked to carry out this monstrous rampage. Until the end of the following combat phase, add 1 to the Attacks characteristic of this model's melee weapons, but all attacks made with this model's melee weapons must target the same enemy unit.

WARSCROLL UPDATE

HERDSTONE WARSCROLL
The following warscroll replaces all versions of this warscroll with an earlier publication date.

Wrought from the Chaos-infused substance of the realms, Herdstones are the sites at which the Beasts of Chaos carry out their savage rituals. As the Greatfrays stampede further into civilised territories, they continue to erect Herdstones, from which the corruptive taint of the anarchic wilds bleeds freely into the land.

FACTION TERRAIN WARSCROLL
HERDSTONE

FACTION TERRAIN: Only Beasts of Chaos armies can include this faction terrain feature.

SET-UP: After territories are determined, you can set up this faction terrain feature wholly within your territory and more than 3" from all objectives and other terrain features. If both players can set up faction terrain features at the same time, they must roll off and the winner chooses who sets up their faction terrain features first.

IMPASSABLE: You cannot move a model over this terrain feature unless it can fly, and you cannot move a model onto this terrain feature or set up a model on this terrain feature (even if it can fly).

Entropic Lodestone: *As the corrupting influence of the Herdstone spreads, buildings, armour and other trappings of civilisation and order begin to crumble to dust, allowing even the crude weapons of the Beasts of Chaos to cut through their defences with ease.*

Improve the Rend characteristic of melee weapons used by all friendly BEASTS OF CHAOS units on the battlefield by 1. From the start of the third battle round, improve the Rend characteristic of melee weapons used by all friendly BEASTS OF CHAOS units on the battlefield by 2 instead of 1.

Locus of Savagery: *A Herdstone marks the domain of the Beasts of Chaos, and in its presence they fight with unfailing vigour.*

After this terrain feature is set up, its range is 12". At the start of each battle round after the first, its range is increased by 6".

If a friendly BEASTS OF CHAOS unit wholly within range of this terrain feature fails a battleshock test, halve the number of models that flee from that unit (rounding down). In addition, if a friendly BEASTS OF CHAOS unit wholly within range of this terrain feature receives the Rally command, you can return 1 slain model to that unit for each 4+ instead of each 6.

WHITE DWARF **25**

OPEN PLAY

If the players are using the Open War battlepack from the *Warhammer Age of Sigmar Core Book*, players using a **BEASTS OF CHAOS** army can use the following rules as well as those found in the battlepack.

BEASTS OF CHAOS TWIST

If the roll on the Twist table is a 1, you can ignore the No Twist result and roll on the following table instead. If both players can roll on a Twist table in this way, so long as those Twist tables are different, each player can roll on their Twist table and both twists are used for the battle (each twist applies to each player, as normal).

BEASTS OF CHAOS TWIST TABLE	
D6	**Twist**
1-3	**Murder of Crows:** *A flock of carrion birds circles above the battlefield, waiting to descend upon the fallen. It is a fell omen for either side, and their commanders will be hard-pressed to maintain discipline.* During this battle, unit champions cannot issue the Inspiring Presence command.
4-6	**Ruinous Rampage:** *Twisting tendrils of Chaotic energy have sunk deep into the earth here, sending the monstrous creatures of the land into an unstoppable frenzy.* During this battle, players can carry out the same monstrous rampage with different **MONSTERS** in the same phase.

BEASTS OF CHAOS RUSE

When you generate your ruse, you can use the following ruse instead of the one you generate on the Ruse table (choose which to use after you have made your roll on the Ruse table).

Summon the Gor-kin: *When the moment is right, the champions of the Greatfrays let loose primal horn-blasts and furious howls, calling upon their fellow beasts to descend upon the battlefield and join the slaughter.*

Once per battle, at the end of your movement phase, you can choose to call the wild. If you do so, you receive 2D6 primordial call points. However, after that, you can receive no further primordial call points for the rest of the battle.

MATCHED PLAY

If the battlepack you are using says that you must pick grand strategies and battle tactics for your army, you can pick from the following lists as well as those found in the battlepack you are using.

GRAND STRATEGIES

After you have picked your army, you can pick the grand strategy below and record it on your army roster.

THE WAY OF THE BEAST
Beasts of Chaos army only.

Protect the Herdstone: *At the heart of every beastman encampment stands a Herdstone, a nexus of dark, atavistic power that the gor-kin will lay down their lives to defend.*

When the battle ends, you complete this grand strategy if there are no enemy units within 9" of your Herdstone and it has not been picked by a successful Smash To Rubble monstrous rampage.

BATTLE TACTICS

At the start of your hero phase, you can pick 1 battle tactic from the list below. You must reveal your choice to your opponent, and if your battle tactic instructs you to pick something, you must tell your opponent what you pick. You have until the end of that turn to complete the battle tactic. You cannot pick the same battle tactic more than once per battle.

HUNTERS OF THE WARPING WILDS
Beasts of Chaos army only.

In the Shadow of the Herdstone: *To sacrifice enemies beneath the horned shadow of the Herdstone is to appease the primal force of ruin and draw its anarchic energies to the battlefield.*

Pick 1 enemy unit within 9" of your Herdstone. You complete this battle tactic if that unit is destroyed during this turn.

Fury of the Wild: *Before the enemy have time to react, the cunning warriors of the beastherd are all around them, hacking them down without hesitation.*

You can pick this tactic only in your first turn. You complete this battle tactic if the model picked to be your general and two or more other friendly **Beasts of Chaos** units are within 3" of an enemy unit at the end of this turn.

Wrath of the Warped Wilds: *Out in the twisted wilderness roam entire packs of furious beast-kin, eager to join the hunts of the Greatfrays and tear apart their hated prey at but a single beckoning call.*

Pick 1 objective controlled by your opponent. You complete this battle tactic at the end of the turn if you control that objective and it is contested by any models in your army that were summoned with the Primordial Call battle trait.

PATH TO GLORY

This section contains rules for using a Beasts of Chaos army in a Path to Glory campaign. It includes additional rules, quests, veteran abilities and unique territories that can only be used by a Beasts of Chaos army.

VETERAN

Each time a BEASTS OF CHAOS unit on your Path to Glory roster gains a veteran ability, you can pick 1 of the veteran abilities from the table below instead of the table found in the Core Book.

BEASTS OF CHAOS VETERAN ABILITIES

Leaders of the Ambush: *As your Brayherd hunts down its enemies and prowls the hidden beastpaths, it is these warriors who lead the way.*

BRAYHERD unit only. This unit can use this veteran ability once per battle in the combat phase of your first turn if it was set up in ambush this battle. Add 1 to the Attacks characteristic of this unit's melee weapons until the end of the phase.

Blood-hungry: *As these brutes gulp down the remains of the enemy, the aura of monstrous hunger that clings to them draws more Bullgors out from the long shadows of the wilderness.*

WARHERD unit only. This unit can use this veteran ability once per battle at the end of the combat phase if it destroyed any enemy units in that phase. You can return D3 slain models to this unit.

Storm-heralds: *Empowered by bolts of dark lightning, these Dragon Ogors race into the fray at the crest of the oncoming storm.*

THUNDERSCORN unit only. This unit can use this veteran ability once per battle at the start of your hero phase if it is more than 3" from all enemy units. If this unit makes a normal move as a result of the Creatures of the Storm battle trait, it can make a normal move of 6" instead of a number of inches equal to the roll.

BEASTS OF CHAOS QUESTS

If your army is a Beasts of Chaos army, you can pick the following quest for your Path to Glory roster.

QUEST
ANARCHY UNLEASHED

With gathering momentum, your bestial warband rampages through the so-called civilised lands. Each victory sees more savage creatures drawn to your banner, until at last nothing will be able to stop your horde from sacking the domains of your foes.

At the end of each Path to Glory battle, add 1 quest point to the progress section of your quest log if you earned a **major victory** or **minor victory**. In addition, while this quest is on your Path to Glory roster, at the start of each Path to Glory battle against another Path to Glory army, you receive a number of primordial call points equal to the number of quest points in your quest log.

Once you have gained 5 quest points, you complete this quest. When you complete this quest, you gain 10 glory points. In addition, when making the first exploration roll in the aftermath sequence of the battle in which you completed this quest, do not roll a D66. Instead, roll a D6 and add 60 to the roll (giving a score of 61-66).

TERRITORIES

When making an exploration roll, if the roll is 61-66, that roll will correspond to a territory on the table below. Alternatively, you can pick 1 result from the Territories table in the Core Book that corresponds to a roll of 21-42.

BEASTS OF CHAOS FACTION TERRITORIES (D66)

61-62 TAINTED DEEPWOODS

Within the twisted shadows of this ancient forest stalk tribes of the gor-kin who can be rallied to your cause and used to bolster your raids upon the forces of civilisation.

When fighting a Path to Glory battle against another Path to Glory army, at the end of the battleshock phase, you can pick 1 friendly **BRAYHERD** unit that is set up in ambush. You can return D6 slain models to that unit.

[Upgrade 10GP] Twisting Pathways: You can pick 2 such units instead of 1.

63-64 WILD MOUNTAINS

Chaos magic swirls around the peaks of these mountains, drawing all manner of monstrosities to bathe in its power. Stamping your dominion upon the region would allow you to bolster your growing beastherd with these powerful creatures.

Increase the **MONSTERS** limit on your order of battle by 2. In addition, in Step 7 of each aftermath sequence, roll a dice. On a 1-5, nothing happens. On a 6, a **MONSTER** is beckoned to join your beastherd. If so, you can add 1 **BEASTS OF CHAOS MONSTER** to your order of battle without spending any glory to do so.

[Upgrade 10GP] Raised Herdstone Upon the Mountain: Increase the limit by 4 instead of 2.

65-66 WARP-NEXUS

This ley line convergence has been blessed by Chaos in its purest form and now seethes with the raw stuff of anarchy. To erect a Herdstone over this font of dark power will assert your dominance for miles in all directions.

You can never have more than 1 territory of this type. This territory has no effect until it is upgraded.

[Upgrade 30GP] Warp-infused Herdstone: When fighting a Path to Glory battle against another Path to Glory army, the range of your Herdstone's Locus of Dark Savagery ability is 18" at the start of the battle.

TO HUNT THE DAWN

The arrogant mortals of Sigmar's hosts dare to defile the sacred Herdstones erected upon the Beastbridge in their desire to claim more lands. You must summon the true children of Chaos to your side and defend these places of primal power.

The Realm of Fire has always been a place of strife. Rarely has this been more true than in the Era of the Beast. Hammerhal Aqsha, that bastion of mortalkind raised amidst the desolation of the Great Parch, echoes constantly to the sound of military preparations. New hosts of Dawnbringers march far and wide, seeking ingress into lands long lost to corruption. Here they strive to establish themselves and draw upon the geomantic energies of Aqshy to use its fiery soul to power arcane devices. Through these mystical wellsprings, they will begin a new life in the reclaimed realms.

But you are the gor-kin, the true children, the Cloven Ones. You are the masters of this wilderness, the horned monsters that struck terror into the ancestors of these upstarts. You will teach them that fear once again. Any who enter your hunting grounds deserve only death, whether delivered in one savage blow or through swift and cunning surprise.

A feral impetus now moves through your soul. The beastherd's Bray-Shamans speak of blood bubbling to the surface across the parched plains, of igneous rocks that tremble and scream in anticipation. The power of ruin calls to you, warning you of the advance of another crusader host. This force has travelled further than many of its kin, heading for the Beastbridge – a stretch of fractured land that links the continent of Bataar to the expanse of the Flamescar Plateau. It has long been inhabited by the gor-kin, a place from which to launch brutal raids into the domains of mortals. Were it to be claimed by the Hammerhalian forces, however, it could, over time, transform into a strong outpost of civilisation that joins the two landmasses and the vile cities raised upon them. This blasphemy cannot be permitted.

Three Herdstones dominate the region around the Beastbridge where the mortals seek to settle. One lies in a swamp, another atop a mountain peak and the third amidst a network of dark sulphur-caverns. All are lodestones of Chaos energy, sending waves of warping magic cascading through the area and giving rise to the many anarchic creatures that dwell in the region. To lay down roots, the Hammerhalians must topple at least two of the Herdstones. You must prevent this at all costs. However, a cunning beast knows how to turn an apparent weakness into an advantage. The mortals' need to cast down your idols will see them drawn along routes that are familiar to you. They will be watched by your packs of ambushing warriors. By successfully harrying the worshippers of the Storm God, you will draw in more creatures of Chaos who recognise your strength and willpower. More importantly, you will feed the lands with the energies of ruin and unlock the true strength of the Herdstones …

INTRODUCTION

On these pages, you will find a campaign arc for 2 players. One player takes the role of the Beasts of Chaos and the other player takes the role of the Cities of Sigmar as you play through a series of battles to decide the fate of the Beastbridge.

WHAT'S A CAMPAIGN ARC?

A campaign arc is a self-contained mini-campaign that can either be played as a standalone campaign or as part of a Path to Glory campaign. This one is designed to last for 2-3 battles, making for a perfect weekend's worth of gaming between 2 players.

FORGING A DIFFERENT NARRATIVE

If you do not have an opponent with a Cities of Sigmar army, you can quickly adapt this campaign to another army. For example, the Dawnbringer Crusade may have a vanguard of Stormcast Eternals, or perhaps it has mercenaries in pay such as the Fyreslayers or Kharadron Overlords. You could also take the rules for this campaign and use it to tell a completely different story, such as a force of Orruk Warclans seeking to ransack three sacred groves of the Sylvaneth.

THE BATTLEPACK

This campaign arc can be played with either the Path to Glory battlepack or the Open War battlepack. If you play through the campaign with Path to Glory armies, there are extra rewards to add to your Path to Glory roster at the end of the campaign.

GETTING READY

One player takes the role of the Beasts of Chaos; the other plays the Cities of Sigmar. There are 3 locations in this campaign (shown on the map), each the site of a Herdstone: Slythemarsh, Harghar's Crown and the Choking Den.

Before the campaign can begin, the Beasts of Chaos player must decide which of the three locations is to be their **primary defence**, which is to be their **secondary defence** and which is to be their **last resort**. To make this decision, the Beasts of Chaos player is encouraged to look at the rewards each of the locations will give to the victor and try to guess where the Cities of Sigmar player is likely to attack (see the location tables overleaf for details). Once the Beasts of Chaos player has made their decision, they should note it down in secret. The campaign is now ready to begin!

PLAYING THE CAMPAIGN

The campaign will consist of 2-3 battles. For the first battle, the Cities of Sigmar player picks 1 of the 3 locations to attack. When making their choice, they are encouraged to both look at the rewards each location gives the victor and to also try to guess where the Beasts of Chaos player has left the weakest point in their defence.

Once the Cities of Sigmar player has chosen the location of the first battle, the Beasts of Chaos player reveals if the location was their primary defence, secondary defence or last resort. This determines how many points the Beasts of Chaos player can spend when picking their army, as follows:

LOCATION TYPE	POINTS OF THE BEASTS OF CHAOS ARMY
PRIMARY DEFENCE	10% more points than the Cities of Sigmar army
SECONDARY DEFENCE	Equal points to the Cities of Sigmar army
LAST RESORT	10% fewer points than the Cities of Sigmar army

FIGHTING THE BATTLE

Each battle in this campaign arc is fought using the same battleplan, 'Sunder the Herdstone', found on page 35. However, depending on the location of the battle, the battleplan will have special rules as noted on the location tables.

If you are using the Open War battlepack, roll on the Twist and Ruse tables as normal, but do not roll on the Map or Victory tables.

After the armies have been picked, fight the battle using the Warhammer Age of Sigmar rules.

THE AFTERMATH

After each battle has been fought, the winner of the battle gains the reward of that location in the next battle of the campaign arc. After the first battle has been fought, the Cities of Sigmar player picks one of the remaining two locations to be the location of the second battle. After the second battle, if either player has won 2 victories, the campaign arc ends and that player is declared the winner. If both players have won 1 victory each, a final battle is fought at the last remaining location, and the winner of that battle is declared the winner of the campaign arc.

REWARDS FOR PATH TO GLORY ARMIES

For players using Path to Glory armies with this campaign arc, they gain the following benefits:

1. In step 3 of the aftermath sequence after each battle, units involved gain a bonus D3 renown points each.

2. The winner of the campaign arc can immediately add 1 artefact of power to their vault. For the Beasts of Chaos, the artefact is an offering given to your Beastlord by the Bray-Shamans in gratitude for empowering the Herdstones with sacrifice. For the Cities of Sigmar, it represents a relic recovered from an ancient site in these long-desecrated lands, now freed from the clutches of Chaos.

LOCATION TABLES

SLYTHEMARSH

Contorted, pale-barked trees dot this mire, constantly writhing and creaking as if in agony, their roots plunging into filthy pools of steaming swamp water. These are the hunting grounds of the Jabberslythes, and they have been shaped into a deranged reflection of these creatures' vile souls. It is said that those foolish enough to tread here soon leave their sanity behind.

SPECIAL RULES

Lost in the Swamp: *The twisting, steam-shrouded paths of this foetid swamp can deceive even the most astute pathfinders, and before long the warriors of the Dawnbringer Crusade may find themselves isolated from their allies and hopelessly lost.*

During deployment, each time a **CITIES OF SIGMAR** unit is set up on the battlefield, first roll a dice. On the roll of a 1 or a 2, that unit is lost in the swamp and is placed to one side instead.

At the end of each of the Cities of Sigmar player's turns, they can roll a dice for each unit lost in the swamp. If the roll is equal to or less than the number of the current battle round, that unit is set up in their territory, wholly within 6" of a battlefield edge and more than 9" from all enemy units.

At the end of the battle, any units lost in the swamp that have not been set up on the battlefield are destroyed.

REWARDS

Beasts of Chaos: If the Beasts of Chaos player wins the battle, in the next battle they can add 3 to charge rolls for friendly units if they were reserve units in ambush that were set up on the battlefield in the same turn.

Cities of Sigmar: If the Cities of Sigmar player wins the battle, once per turn in the next battle, 1 **CITIES OF SIGMAR** unit can receive the All-out Attack command without the command being issued and without a command point being spent.

THE CHOKING DEN

Further west across the Beastbridge, the mountain passes turn thick with choking ash-clouds. Sulphurous plumes of smoke rise from volcanoes to darken the sky, belched forth from caverns that ring with the howl of subterranean abominations. Deep within this region is said to lie a Herdstone that siphons and corrupts arcane energy from the depths of Aqshy. To purify it, the Dawners must venture into the warren of gas-filled caverns below the earth.

SPECIAL RULES

Subterranean Battlefield: *Into the darkness did the Dawnbringer Crusade descend, to cast down the Herdstone found at this mountain's core.*

Use the Tunnel Fighting rules for this battle (Core Book, pg 354). In addition, do not roll off as instructed in the Monstrous Denizen rule. Instead, the Beasts of Chaos player is considered to have won the roll-off.

Sulphuric Haze: *So thick and dense are the drifting clouds of sulphuric gas within these caverns that it is almost impossible to make out an enemy up ahead.*

Models are not visible to each other if the distance between them is more than 12". This includes the Herdstone.

REWARDS

Beasts of Chaos: If the Beasts of Chaos player wins the battle, in the next battle, they can include a Ravening Direflock, a Doomblast Dirgehorn and a Wildfire Taurus in their army without them counting towards their points limit.

Cities of Sigmar: If the Cities of Sigmar player wins the battle, in the next battle, add 1 to casting rolls for **CITIES OF SIGMAR WIZARDS**.

HARGHAR'S CROWN

These mountains take their name from the legendary Beastlord Harghar. If the Beasts of Chaos can hold the towering Herdstone erected on the flank of the greatest peak, it will serve as a rallying point for the gor-kin to repel the hated trespassers. For the Dawners, to lay low this icon of ruin will send a stark message that the foul beasts cannot stop their crusade of reconquest.

SPECIAL RULES

Rock-hard Monolith: *Carved from smoky quartz formed even before the Age of Myth, this Herdstone is impervious to all but the strongest of attacks.*

Only wound rolls of an unmodified 6 are successful for attacks that target the Herdstone.

Falling Rocks: *The cliffs of the western rise have been loosened by the advance up the mountains of the Dawnbringer Crusade and now threaten to send boulders plummeting down upon the battlefield.*

At the end of each turn, roll a dice for each unit within 9" of the western battlefield edge. On a 1, that unit suffers D6 mortal wounds.

REWARDS

Beasts of Chaos: If the Beasts of Chaos player wins the battle, in the next battle, the range of the Herdstone's Locus of Savagery ability is 12" at the start of the battle.

Cities of Sigmar: If the Cities of Sigmar player wins the battle, once per turn in the next battle, a **CITIES OF SIGMAR** unit can receive the Rally command without the command being issued and without a command point being spent.

BATTLEPLAN
SUNDER THE HERDSTONE

As the Dawnbringer Crusade marches across the Beastbridge, they set out to lay low the Chaotic monoliths that spread corruption across the lands. But the Beasts of Chaos will grant them no easy passage and fight bitterly to repel the hated forces of civilisation.

THE ARMIES

The Beasts of Chaos player is the **defender**. The Cities of Sigmar player is the **attacker**. Armies are picked following all other rules outlined in the battlepack being used.

THE BATTLEFIELD

The players roll off. The winner sets up the battlefield's terrain features and then the other player chooses which long edge of the battlefield is the northern edge.

After the terrain features have been set up, starting with the player who won the roll-off, each player picks 1 terrain feature and rolls on the Mysterious Terrain table (core rules, 28.1.3) to determine which scenery rule applies to that terrain feature during the battle.

FACTION TERRAIN

The Beasts of Chaos player must set up a Herdstone. The location of the Herdstone is shown on the map. Remove any other terrain features that prevent the Herdstone being placed in its location.

DEPLOYMENT

The attacker sets up first, wholly within their territory. The defender sets up their army second, wholly within their territory, and more than 9" from all enemy units.

BATTLE LENGTH

The battle lasts for 5 battle rounds.

FIRST TURN

The players roll off and the winner picks which player takes the first turn in the first battle round.

THE LOCATION OF BATTLE

The location of the battle will determine additional special rules used in this battleplan (see pages 33 and 34).

SUNDERING THE HERDSTONE

The Herdstone is treated as an enemy model by the Cities of Sigmar player. This means it can be targeted by attacks and other abilities. It is not treated as a friendly model by the Beasts of Chaos player.

The Herdstone has a Save characteristic of 2+. Keep a record of how many wounds are allocated to it each turn.

If the Herdstone is affected by a successful Smash To Rubble, D6 wounds are allocated to the Herdstone instead of the normal effect.

At the end of each turn, roll a number of dice as shown on the table below determined by the points limit for the Cities of Sigmar army this battle. If the roll is less than the number of wounds allocated to the Herdstone in that turn, the Herdstone is **damaged**.

Points Limit	Dice
<1000	3D6
1000-1499	4D6
1500-1999	5D6
2000+	6D6

The first time the Herdstone becomes damaged, nothing happens. The second time it is damaged, the Beasts of Chaos become enraged: add 1 to the Attacks characteristic of the melee weapons **BEASTS OF CHAOS** units are armed with. The third time it is damaged, it is **sundered** and the battle ends.

GLORIOUS VICTORY

When the battle ends, if the Herdstone has been sundered, the Cities of Sigmar player wins a **major victory**. Otherwise, the Beasts of Chaos player wins a **major victory**.

BEASTS OF CHAOS TERRITORY	THE HERDSTONE	BEASTS OF CHAOS TERRITORY
	CITIES OF SIGMAR TERRITORY	

A TALE OF FOUR WARLORDS

THE ORIGINAL WHITE DWARF * A TALE OF FOUR WARLORDS * 2021

The Mortal Realms are in turmoil following the Shyish Necroquake, and the fate of countless lands hangs in the balance. Now, four warlords march to war. Will the forces of Chaos prevail, or will the armies of Order bring light to the realms once more?

THE ORIGINAL WHITE DWARF * A TALE OF FOUR WARLORDS * 2021

SLAVES TO DARKNESS

HEDONITES OF SLAANESH

LUMINETH REALM-LORDS

CITIES OF SIGMAR

Back in the mists of time, before Chaos descended upon the Mortal Realms, four warlords donned their armour and took up arms. Two were champions of Chaos, intent on corrupting all they touched; two were heroes of Order, ready to defend all that was good and just. Over the last year, they have drawn warriors to themselves like axe-wielding moths to magical flames, culminating in four huge armies. And yes, this is the culmination, because we have come to the end of this series of A Tale of Four Warlords! Over the next few pages, you'll get to see their armies in all their glory and read their thoughts on a year of hobbying. Here's a brief summary of what they've been up to recently:

From atop his perch in the Vertiginous Peaks, the Spirit of the Mountain known as Martyn Lyon has summoned the most powerful being he can find (and paint in a two-month period …) to join his Lumineth Realm-lords. Gaze in wonder upon Archmage Teclis and Celennar, Spirit of Hysh!

Nomad Prince and devoted servant of Morrda Rich Packer has called upon Sigmar to aid him in his time of need. In this final article of the series, his Cities of Sigmar army is joined by chariots, heroes and Sigmar's vengeance made manifest in the form of the Celestant-Prime.

Miyuki Foulkes is our resident Lord of Ruin and dedicated servant of the Dark Gods. Having drawn together the three armies of the Uem-nai River, she now plans to march on the lands of mortals and lay waste to all before her. The monsters she's painted for this month's challenge will surely help with that!

Lord of Excess and master of seduction Calum McPherson has made a right meal of his models this month. No, he hasn't messed them up (or eaten them!), but rather he's painted the Lord of Gluttony and food connoisseur himself, Glutos Orscollion. Calum reckons he'll be a sweet treat for the other warlords to face. We're not so sure!

Top: The Augurs of Morrda are charged by a unit of Gore-gruntas and utterly pulverised. Apparently they will go through bone like butter.
Bottom: The Shields of Morrda find themselves surrounded by Gore-gruntas, Brutes and Brakkus the Megaboss. It takes several turns of intense fighting for them to break out.

THE WAR OF CONQUEST BEGINS!

For this edition of A Tale of Four Warlords, our four hobbyists will mostly be playing narrative games, the rules for which can be found on page 302 of the new *Warhammer Age of Sigmar Core Book*. They are also forging heroes of their very own using the Anvil of Apotheosis rules as presented on page 56 of the *General's Handbook* 2020.

For each article in the series, our warlords need to paint at least 500 points for their army, which can include any combination of units, heroes and war machines they like, though their force should still be able to fit into a battle roster. By the end of the challenge, they will each have a sizeable collection.

As we come to the last article of the series, most of the warlords have been focused on completing their last few models. Miyuki, Martyn and Calum have all been working on large models and have hidden themselves away in hobby rooms, studies and dungeons (we'll let you decide who was in which room) to concentrate on getting them finished.

Rich, however, has taken to the gaming table once more to do battle with his friend and semi-regular opponent, Megaboss Richard Sherlock. Earlier in this series, Rich and Richard fought the first two battles in a three-battle campaign they'd devised, and they were determined to conclude it before this final article. Having each won a game, they set about playing the final game in their campaign, which was fought around the Bridge of Axes – a realmgate that Richard painted specially for the game. Who won the series-deciding final game? We'll let Rich tell you the outcome later!

LUMINETH REALM-LORDS

DEFENDERS OF MOUNT AVALENOR

The banners have been called, the mountain spirits have been appeased, and the luminaries have been consulted – the warriors of Ymetrica march to war! And at their head stands the mighty Teclis, the latest and greatest of Martyn's creations.

MARTYN LYON

Over the course of this challenge, Martyn has painted fifty-two infantry models, three behemoths and a spell. Of his fifteen units, nine of them are leaders. Never let it be said that the Lumineth Realm-lords don't have a solid command structure!

Martyn: So, this is it. The summit reached. Glory attained. Immortality achieved. After what feels like an eternity, we've finally reached the end of the series. And what a series it's been! This journey was started before the harrowing events of Spring 2020, and it has seen us all attempt to maintain some semblance of normality through this time by painting and collecting armies for Warhammer Age of Sigmar. I don't think I need to tell you how helpful having a hobby like this has been over the last few years. I'm sure we've all needed Warhammer recently more than ever.

But what of the armies? I have the privilege of working alongside the Age of Sigmar photography team as they produce the battletomes, so I saw the Lumineth long before they were announced, and it was love at first sight. Having flirted with almost every army of the Mortal Realms since Warhammer Age of Sigmar was announced, I could never quite settle on any one faction. Then the shining light of the Lumineth came into focus, and I knew I'd finally found the army for me.

I wrote a rough list at the very beginning – the Dwarfers were keen for us to understand the commitment required for the challenge that lay before us! On paper, it all seemed straightforward. A few units here, a couple of characters there. In reality, my interest is not so rigid, and I often found myself deviating from the intended path.

My style of collecting is very reactive – I fall in love with a new miniature and want to work on it straight away, at the expense of the miniature I *should* have been painting that month.

THE LORD OF THE LUMINETH

One thing was clear from the beginning, though – my final centrepiece would be Archmage Teclis and Celennar, Spirit of Hysh. What a magnificent crowning achievement this would be to my lengthy campaign. At first, Teclis looked quite daunting; I'm not sure the photographs really get across how big he is! I was advised to paint him in sub-assemblies, and luckily the kit is designed so well that this is really straightforward. I kept him in the following pieces: the base, Celennar, Teclis and his cloak.

As far as the painting went, I knew my colour scheme pretty well at this point, so Teclis was easy enough to work on. I did consider painting Celennar a darker blue (or even black), but ultimately I ended up going with a similar colour to the miniature on the box cover. This was achieved using Skrag Brown – a lovely colour that I hadn't really used previously. The wings were then darkened using Wyldwood Contrast paint. Teclis was painted predominantly in Lothern Blue, and his metallic elements were painted Ironbreaker with a shade of thinned Akhelian Green to tie him into the rest of the army.

THE 3,000-POINT MARK

Well, it's safe to say that I easily hit the 3,000-point mark, thanks in part to a couple of small points changes! The crazy thing is there are so many models in the Lumineth range that I didn't even get to explore the Hurakan side of things before the challenge was over. I reckon if I added in one of each Hurakan unit, my army would easily surpass 5,000 points. Most of the time, my army will be led by the Light of Eltharion or Avalenor as, at 740 points, I find Teclis a little expensive for your average 2,000-point game. I look forward to using him in my larger battles, though.

Units	Size	Role/Ally	Pts
Teclis	1	Leader, Behemoth	740
The Light of Eltharion	1	Leader	250
Scinari Cathallar	1	Leader	145
Avalenor, the Stoneheart King	1	Leader, Behemoth	415
Vanari Bannerblade	1	Leader	120
Alarith Stonemage	1	Leader	130
Scinari Calligrave	1	Leader	115
Scinari Loreseeker	1	Leader	170
Converted Vanari Bannerblade	1	Leader	160
Spirit of the Mountain	1	Behemoth	375
Vanari Auralan Wardens	20	Battleline	290
Alarith Stoneguard	10	Battleline	240
Vanari Auralan Sentinels	10	Battleline	150
Vanari Bladelords	5	Battleline	130
Rune of Petrification	1	Endless Spell	75
			3505

Teclis in all his luminous majesty! I knew right from the start of the challenge that he would be the centrepiece miniature of my collection. How could he not be?!

WHAT'S NEXT...
No more aelves for a while! I'm going to work on a few other projects for a bit, including a heavily weathered Dark Angels kill team. However, the next time *White Dwarf* runs A Tale of Four Warlords for Warhammer 40,000, I'm going to try to paint along at the same time. I like the look of Dark Angels. Or maybe Tyranids. Then again, I've always loved Aeldari. But then there's Orks, or possibly ...

SLAVES TO DARKNESS

UEM-NAI'S WRATH

Three Chaos Warlords, united in purpose, lead a vast army from the lands of the Uem-nai. As their hordes march forth to bring wrath and ruin to the Mortal Realms, they are joined by Miyuki's latest creations: a savage warband and a couple of monsters.

MIYUKI FOULKES

Over the course of this immense challenge, Miyuki has painted twenty infantry models, twenty-nine cavalry, seven monsters or war machines, three spells and the Dark Master himself. Her house is now marked for all time with an eight-pointed star.

Miyuki: This is it! The full force of Uem-nai's Wrath has gathered, ready to wreak havoc on the Mortal Realms. Aimed at taking down as many Dawner settlements and caravans as possible, Archaon wants the three brothers to ensure there are no new Cities of Sigmar established anywhere in the Mortal Realms. With the majority of the force mounted on horseback, they will cover great distances and make it near impossible for any settlers to escape. They will put fear into anyone who even considers leaving the safety of an established city. None will survive.

THE FINAL FORCE

To finish off the challenge, I've included a new unit and two big-hitters. Phan-koon, the Fomoroid Crusher, is from the lowlands near Motoharu's territory. He is well known for his rages when he sees Khayn Shaimurah, who was once his captor and kept him as one of his pets. Jaimus, the Ogroid Myrmidon, stalks the bridges that cross the Uem-nai throughout Takamoto's lands, looking for worthy opponents to test his skills. He has joined the warband to continue his search across the Mortal Realms. The Spire Tyrants warband – from the mountainous area of Takakage – are unnaturally unaffected by the cold and terrible conditions of the mountains. They are known for their ability to hunt down and punish escaped slaves from the mines. With their help, no one will escape Uem-nai's Wrath!

PAINTING

I loosely based my colour schemes for the Ogroid Myrmidon and Fomoroid Crusher on the box images but with a few extra colours to tie them into the three brothers' forces (such as Phan-koon's gold shoulder pad). I painted both monsters with a similar skin tone, using Wraithbone as a basecoat followed by a wash of Reikland Fleshshade. Then I applied a layer of Pallid Wych Flesh followed by White Scar. This gives them a pale and sickly look, like you would expect from creatures who live around Uem-nai.

TAKING ON THE CHALLENGE

I cannot believe that I managed to reach 3,000 points! This was a huge project, but I really don't feel it took a whole year – it seems a lot shorter. I never thought I could finish an army of that size, but I didn't tell the *White Dwarf* team that at the start! I really appreciate all the support I received from the experienced players I talked to: the other guys in A Tale of Four Warlords, who were kind and very understanding; my friend Masahito (who owns his own store in Sapporo, Japan), who gave me lots of painting and building advice; and the shop staff in the UK and Japan. My co-worker Satoru also gave me lots of advice for my custom hero, while my Twitter followers and family gave me encouragement and praise. This hobby and this challenge have helped me meet so many people and build my confidence.

THE 3,000-POINT MARK

My husband and I have been playing small 500-1,000-point games in the evening after the kids are asleep. I really want to play a game with the full force, but the kitchen table is needed for dinner! Getting in big games is definitely one of the biggest challenges I have faced. I'm already looking forward to using Phan-koon's Rampage ability as I'm just going to charge him into combat as much as I can. Meanwhile, Jaimus can keep the Spire Tyrants in check with his Pit Marshal ability. I'm looking forward to leaving Paul in charge of the kids while I get out to play some games!

Units	Size	Role/Ally	Pts
Be'lakor	1	Leader, Behemoth	360
Khayn Shaimurah, Chaos Lord on Karkadrak	1	Leader	225
Chakatoone, Chaos Sorcerer	1	Leader, Behemoth	390
Darkoath Warqueen	1	Leader	90
Jaimus, Ogroid Myrmidon	1	Leader	135
Chaos Warriors	10	Battleline	200
Chaos Knights	5	Battleline	170
Chaos Knights	10	Battleline	340
Chaos Chariots	3	Battleline	315
Chaos Marauder Horsemen	10	Battleline	220
Spire Tyrants	9		70
Varanguard	3		280
Mindstealer Sphiranx	1		95
Phan-koon, Fomoroid Crusher	1		110
Realmscourge Rupture	1	Endless Spell	85
Eightfold Doom-Sigil	1	Endless Spell	50
Darkfire Daemonrift	1	Endless Spell	100
			3235

Phan-koon is known to fly into a rage when he sees Khayn Shaimurah, who was once his captor and kept him as one of his pets. Jaimus is more of a free spirit!

THE LAST OF THE TYRANTS

To bring my collection full circle, the colour scheme for the Spire Tyrants matches that of the Start Collecting! box I painted at the beginning of the challenge. This time I copied the colour scheme in the building guide closely. It was interesting seeing how much my painting has improved, and I was most surprised at how quickly I was able to paint them compared to when I first started. I also played with the colours a bit, as I have a lot more confidence now. I tried different skin tones, and I spent a lot more time highlighting the black. The most difficult part was the eyes. I was lucky to get a tip from a Twitter follower who suggested painting them black first then two dots of white, leaving a black line in the middle. It was so much easier to paint them this way.

WHAT'S NEXT...
I'm going to keep practising my painting! I've really enjoyed learning new painting skills, and I want to try out lots more. I have a few plans for Warcry in the future (I need to paint some scenery for it so that I can play some games with my Spire Tyrants), but I also want to paint some of the new Death Korps of Krieg models for Warhammer 40,000 Kill Team. I quite like the small skirmish games.

CITIES OF SIGMAR

THE ORDER OF MORRDA

Deep within the heart of Hallowstone Hold, a vast army of men, aelves and duardin stands ready for war. As they prepare to battle the dark forces of Chaos, they are joined by one of Sigmar's own – the mighty Celestant-Prime. Rich tells all.

RICH PACKER

Over the course of this series, Rich has painted 140 infantry models, five cavalry, four large monsters or war machines, a Celestant-Prime and three spells. That's one model every two-and-a-bit days. We've all chipped in to buy him a set of new brushes.

Rich: Well, after over a year of building and painting, the Order of Morrda have grown from a mere idea to a respectable host. Some long nights have gone into this! A lot of us have long-suffering partners (a.k.a. Warhammer Widows), so I must thank my wife for her encouragement and patience. I've promised her I'll take a month off now and make her many, many cups of tea.

THE CELESTANT-PRIME

The Anvils of the Heldenhammer are allies of the Order of Morrda, and in times of extreme need, the Celestant-Prime will smite the most belligerent of their foes. Whenever he appears to aid them, his grim countenance bears a striking resemblance to Luther Gottfried, a veteran knight of the World-that-Was and devoted servant of Morrda. I started this conversion very early in the project, so I'm really happy, after over a year in the waiting, to have it finished. I like how he is glaring imperiously down at the enemy as spirits under the protection of Morrda swirl around him, wavy daggers in hand.

THE SHRIKES OF MORRDA

These are Scourgerunner Chariots, and while I made the crew of two of the chariots match the Shields of Morrda Eternal Guard (whose flanks it is their duty to protect), I converted the High Beastmaster to have more of a Morrda theme. The sorceress at the prow is Magdalena the Cursed,

Priestess of Journeys, and the bow-wielding skeleton at her back is Khauron, brother of Lauchon the Soulseeker.

ANKU, PRIEST OF GRAVEYARDS

Anku, the Priest of Graveyards, is the skull-masked sorcerer whose retinue are the Shades of Morrda. Their role is to patrol the mausoleums of Hallowstone Hold and slay the beasts that might try to defile them. They also act as executioners when those who have committed crimes refuse to atone by joining the retinue of Helena Bonsanté. The Shrouds of Morrda (the Shadow Warriors seen in previous articles) aspire to join their ranks, with both the Shrouds and Shades wearing black cloaks. Anku is converted from a Battlemage with the addition of a skull-faced head taken from the Executioners kit. Like many members of the Order, he carries a scythe.

FINAL THOUGHTS

So what am I going to take away from this experience? Well, it's fair to say that I've never painted for so long or so consistently before! Then again, we were all stuck at home with plenty of spare time! But the last year has taught me that playing games is what really fuels my desire to build and paint more models. The few games that I managed to play really energised me and kept me going, and I can't wait to play some more with the Order of Morrda.

THE 3,000-POINT MARK

I finally added a custom character to my force (based on the old Anvil of Apotheosis rules from the *General's Handbook* 2020)! Alissia Tull is a gifted huntress and has a natural affinity with the winds of magic. She's a Champion worth 19 Destiny points with Human ancestry, armed with a bow and sword. She has the Mage archetype with the Wildfire spell (good against larger units). Plus, with Sharpened Edge, 3x Ferocity, Weapon Master and Superior Strength, she's firing five shots with her bow hitting on 2+, wounding on 3+, with -1 Rend and Damage 2. This should be enough to scare some of the squishier wizards.

Units	Size	Role/Ally	Pts
Torallion Leafstar, Nomad Prince	1	Leader	110
Helena Bonsanté, Sorceress	1	Leader	95
Torannion Leafstar, Anointed on Frostheart Phoenix	1	Leader, Behemoth	315
Celestant-Prime	1	Leader	325
Anku, Battlemage	1	Leader	115
Alissia Tull	1	Leader	190
Okri Durragsson, Runelord	1	Leader	100
Dreamwalkers, Phoenix Guard	10		175
Dreadknights, Phoenix Guard	10		175
Blackhearts, Darkshards	10	Battleline	115
Doomsayers, Sisters of the Watch	10	Battleline	180
Limbwithers, Sisters of the Watch	10	Battleline	180
Shrouds of Morrda, Shadow Warriors	10		120
The Shields of Morrda, Eternal Guard	30	Battleline	375
The Augurs of Morrda, Sisters of the Thorn	5	Battleline	130
Tree-Revenants	5		80
Knakkarbokkaz, Longbeards	10	Battleline	105
Zharriskazagal-duk, Irondrakes	20		320
The Oathfists, Irondrakes	10		160
Shrikes of Morrda	3		240
Quicksilver Swords	1	Endless Spell	90
Malevolent Maelstrom	1	Endless Spell	65
Emerald Lifeswarm	1	Endless Spell	60
			3820

This month's painting was a little more random than other months. I basically picked all the cool stuff I'd not yet had the time to paint!

THE BRIDGE OF AXES

I couldn't end this series without playing the final game of the campaign I've been playing against the orruks of Richard Sherlock. At the Bridge of Axes, the Gore-gruntas struck hard and fast, obliterating my Sisters of the Thorn and almost wiping out my thirty Eternal Guard. However, the Sisters of the Watch slew Brakkus the Megaboss with a flurry of blue-fire arrows while Torallion tore through Richard's units. It was the closest game we've fought in the twenty years we've been playing each other. With clever last-turn play, the use of Rally to bring a couple of models back and a well-placed Quicksilver Swords spell, Richard made the game hinge on the very last dice roll. I had to roll two dice and not get any 1s. Let's just say the Order of Morrda is now plotting its revenge.

WHAT'S NEXT...

The Order of Morrda is not complete (what collection ever is?). I have several units undercoated and awaiting their turn to be painted. I'm also going to return to my Hallowheart army and flesh out the Lore of Life and Lore of Beasts components in a Path to Glory campaign with Richard Sherlock, inspired by the novel *Dark Harvest*. The end goal is to have one of every Cities of Sigmar unit painted!

HEDONITES OF SLAANESH

THE HOST OF EXCESS

Driven by an unquenchable desire to inflict pain and pleasure upon their foes, the warriors of the Host of Excess are hungry for battle. Even more so now that they've been joined by Calum's latest creation - the ever-famished Glutos Orscollion.

CALUM MCPHERSON

Over the last year and a bit, Calum has painted forty-five infantry models, three monsters, six cavalry (seven, if Syll'Esske counts as a mounted model!) and three Fiends of Slaanesh that defy categorisation. He is sinfully proud of his achievements.

Calum: With this being the last month of the challenge, I knew I had to bring out the big guns. Or rather, big guts … I'd always planned to finish the series with Glutos Orscollion, which is exactly what I've done!

LORD OF GLUTTONY

I approached painting the model in multiple parts: the palanquin, Glutos himself, each of his accompanying entourage and then the two monsters pulling the whole thing along. This made it much easier to break my time up into manageable chunks and not be overwhelmed by the sheer amount of stuff I had to paint that was, in effect, just one model!

I began from the bottom up and started with the palanquin. I used some airbrush marbling effects (more on that opposite) to achieve the look I wanted, then used Screamer Pink and Sycorax Bronze to tie the palanquin into the rest of my force. I used the same shading on the metal (Guilliman Flesh) as I did for the Myrmidesh Painbringers and my other mortals.

Next, I painted the big guys pulling the palanquin along. I wanted their skin to look almost stone-like, as if they were golems, so I basecoated it Rakarth Flesh then washed it heavily with thinned Mechanicus Standard Grey to give it the stone effect I was looking for. I glazed their scars

with Druchii Violet, then added highlights of Rakarth Flesh to finish them off.

For Glutos, I painted his trousers to match those worn by Syll'Esske in the very first article (*these guys co-ordinate all their evening wear* – Ed), using Night Lords Blue and Blue Horror to match the colours. I wanted his skin to be darker than the model on the box front, so I used the same techniques I had on Syll'Esske but swapped the paints around to be a few tones darker, with the main midtone being Bloodreaver Flesh.

The rest of the characters are painted using the same techniques that I've used across the rest of the army. I think this model ties the force together with all its different aspects.

FINAL THOUGHTS

This journey has been an incredibly enjoyable experience. I've built and painted one of my favourite armies for a series of articles I grew up idolising and never thought I would have the opportunity to be involved in. The past eighteen months have been incredibly difficult for a lot of people, and I feel this challenge has really helped me personally. This hobby has an incredible escapism to it that is always great to get into whether it is through painting, playing or reading the background. Now I just need to prepare myself for the final showdown!

THE 3,000-POINT MARK

My combined army of mortals and daemons easily exceeds the 3,000-point target, which is extremely satisfying. As the latest addition to the force, Glutos is a bit of an unknown quantity right now. He's the most complex unit in the army in terms of the things he can do as he's a powerful wizard, a combat monster, he can buff and protect nearby units … and that's just the start! I need to play a few games with him to see how he will affect my units and my overall army composition. It might mean that I need to add new units to my collection in the future.

Units	Size	Battlefield Role	Pts
Syll'Esske, the Vengeful Allegiance	1	Leader	210
Sigvald	1	Leader	265
Glutos Orscollion	1	Leader, Behemoth	475
Keeper of Secrets	1	Leader, Behemoth	420
Lord of Pain	1	Leader	155
Champion on Steed of Slaanesh	1	Leader	180
Daemonettes	10	Battleline	140
Daemonettes	10	Battleline	140
Myrmidesh Painbringers	10	Battleline	320
Blissbarb Archers	10	Battleline	180
Fiends	3		200
Slickblade Seekers	5		230
Warstomper Mega-Gargant	1	Behemoth, Mercenary	470
			3385

Glutos completes my triumvirate of large centrepiece models, sitting comfortably alongside my Keeper of Secrets and my Warstomper Mega-Gargant.

SIMPLE DECADENCE

For the marble effect on the palanquin I used a simple hobby trick that I saw in *White Dwarf* about a year ago. First I applied a coat of Incubi Darkness to the whole area. Then I took some dried out baby wipes, stretched and tore them up, and laid them over the model. This forms the stencil for the marble patterning.

I airbrushed Kabalite Green over the baby wipe, being careful not to move it during the process. Once the Kabalite Green was dry, I used the airbrush once again to apply a thin layer of Ulthuan Grey followed by White Scar. Once the layers were fully dry, I removed the baby wipe to find lovely colour gradation, marbling and veins created by the shredded fibres of the baby wipes.

WHAT'S NEXT...

I would like to add a few more Slaanesh daemons to my force so that I can field a full daemon army in the future. Perhaps I'll expand the mortal side of my army with some more Battleline units. For the moment, though, I plan to paint some models for Warhammer 40,000. I have my Death Guard to think about, but I also want to paint some of those fantastic new Black Templars models.

1

2

3

4

LUMINETH REALM-LORDS

DEFENDERS OF MOUNT AVALENOR

SLAVES TO DARKNESS

UEM-NAI'S WRATH

THE ORDER OF MORRDA

HEDONITES OF SLAANESH
THE HOST OF EXCESS

OUT ON THE RANGE
(OF THONDIA)

The Realm of Beasts is a dangerous place, where wild beasts and terrifying monsters roam free, and even the land itself hungers for flesh. Will your Warcry warband enter these ever-hungry and ever-deadly lands in search of wondrous treasures? If 'yes', read on!

In the Age of Sigmar, the forces of Order vie for supremacy against their opposites – Chaos, Death and Destruction. Comprising uncountable civilisations, tribes, worshippers and monsters, these Grand Alliances clash over the vast and untameable Mortal Realms.

The Mortal Realm of Ghur – the land of predator and prey, bestial hunger and unquenchable savagery – has been home to some of the most vicious clashes to date. In the region known as Thondia, crusades are launched into the wilderness to create new cities and settlements for the forces of Order. These pioneers meet fierce resistance from the local flora and fauna; when army scouts, skirmishers, and more besides clash, they must deal with the innumerable threats presented by the inhospitable lands.

G reetings, traveller. So you've decided to risk life and limb exploring the realm of Ghur, have you? Well, better you than me. Everything in that realm seeks to eat everything else, so you'd best be bringing the fiercest warriors you can find to keep you alive. What's that? Thondia? Well. Best of luck to you, my friend, for I've heard that the wars that rage there are amongst the fiercest in all the Mortal Realms. Still, there is perhaps some wisdom I can share. After all, I didn't lose three limbs, an eye and most of my courage in that savage place and make it back here alive on sheer good fortune! Get me an ale, and I'll regale you with everything you need to know about the various hazards, pitfalls and, of course, treasures that await you on your journeys!

THE RULES

If you wish for your Warcry battles to take place in Thondia, it couldn't be simpler. Set up a battle according to the Core Book (pg 36-37), but change steps 3 and 4 as instructed below. In addition, the Thondian Savagery rule applies to all fighters.

THONDIAN SAVAGERY

In Thondia, every kind of beast is just that bit bigger or more vicious.

Add 1 to the Toughness characteristic of fighters with the ☗ runemark.

3. VICTORY CONDITION

Roll a dice. On a 1-4, roll another dice and consult chart A to generate a victory condition for your battle in Thondia. On a 5-6, roll a D3 and consult chart B.

D6	CHART A
1	**APEX PREDATOR** *Only the greatest hunter can survive long in Thondia.* If there is no Apex Predator on the battlefield, after a fighter's attack action takes down an enemy fighter, that fighter becomes the Apex Predator. After a fighter's Attack action takes down the Apex Predator, that fighter becomes the Apex Predator. The battle ends after four battle rounds. When the battle ends, the warband that has the Apex Predator is the winner. If neither warband has the Apex Predator, the battle is a draw.
2	**THE UNTAMED RITUAL** *Each warband is attempting a powerful ritual that will wake a nearby behemoth and leash it under their control. It is a perilous endeavour, but one worth the risk.* Starting with the player that won the priority roll, players alternate placing objectives until they have placed 3 objectives each. Each objective can be placed anywhere on the battlefield more than 4" from the battlefield edge and any other objectives. At the end of each battle round, players score 1 ritual point for each objective they control. Each time an enemy fighter is taken down within 3" of an objective controlled by another player, that player scores 2 ritual points. The first player to score 12 ritual points is the winner. If both players score 12 ritual points at the same time, the battle is a draw. The battle ends after four battle rounds. If, when the battle ends, neither player has scored 12 ritual points, the player that has scored the most ritual points is the winner. If both players have scored the same number of ritual points, the battle is a draw.
3	**FEASTING PITS** *While there is no shortage of predators in Thondia, sometimes easy prey can be hard to find. Then, when all else fails, desperate warbands look to their enemies to provide a worthy feast.* Each time a fighter is taken down, the controlling player places an objective within 1" of that fighter before removing them from the battlefield. Once six objectives are on the battlefield, no more objectives are placed. The battle ends after four battle rounds. When the battle ends, the player that controls the most objectives is the winner. If both players hold the same number of objectives, the game is a draw.
4	**SNAPPER TENDING** *Tending Thondian snappers, which are highly valued for their succulent flesh and rich fur, is as lucrative as it is lethal.* Starting with the player that won the priority roll, players alternate placing objectives until they have placed 3 objectives each. Each objective can be placed anywhere on the battlefield more than 4" from the battlefield edge and any other objectives. At the end of each battle round, players score 1 tending point for each objective they control. Then, allocate damage points equal to the battle round number to each fighter within 3" of an objective marker. The first player to score 12 tending points is the winner. If both players score 12 tending points at the same time, the battle is a draw. The battle ends after four battle rounds. When the battle ends, if neither player has scored 12 tending points, the player that has scored the most tending points is the winner. If both players have scored the same number of tending points, the battle is a draw.
5	**CHASE THEM DOWN!** *Cornered prey is elusive indeed. To it catch it, the predator must always think one step ahead.* Place 1 objective in the centre of the battlefield, on the battlefield floor. If it is necessary to move terrain in order to be able to do this, then do so. Each time a fighter moves within 3" of the objective, that fighter's Move action is paused, and a straight line is drawn from the center of the fighter's base through the center of the objective. Move the objective 6" along that line away from the fighter, as if the objective were a flying fighter. The objective always moves onto, and ends its move on, the highest platform possible. If it would move off the battlefield, it instead ends its move at the edge of the battlefield. Then the move action is unpaused and continues. If an objective moves within 1" of a fighter, that fighter has slain the objective – the battle ends and the player controlling that fighter is the winner. The battle ends after four battle rounds. When the battle ends, if no fighter has slain the objective, the battle is a draw.

	MOULDSCUTTLE HARVEST
6	*The hideous mouldscuttle of Thondia is renowned for the wide variety of tinctures and remedies that can be made from it. Unfortunately, it tends to move around quite quickly, especially for a plant, zipping down tunnels and holes as soon as its tendrils are cut.* Starting with the player that won the priority roll, players alternate placing objectives until they have placed 3 objectives each. Each objective can be placed anywhere on the battlefield floor more than 4" from the battlefield edge and any other objectives. At the end of each battle round, players score 1 mould point for each objective they control. Then, move each objective 4" along the battlefield floor in a direct line towards the center of the battlefield, ignoring terrain. Once an objective reaches the center of the battlefield, remove it. The battle ends after four battle rounds. When the battle ends, the player that has scored the most mould points is the winner. If both players have scored the same number of mould points, the battle is a draw.

D3	CHART B
1	THE NEVER-ENDING HUNT *To prosper in the realm of predator and prey, the hunt can never truly end.* The players roll off, and the winner chooses who is the attacker and who is the defender. After setting up the battle, the attacker chooses one enemy fighter that is on the battlefield, then the defender does the same. The chosen fighter is that player's Prey. Each time a player's Prey is taken down, they pick another enemy fighter to be the Prey. The battle ends after four battle rounds. When the battle ends, the winner is the player of whichever warband has taken down the most Prey. If both warbands have taken down the same number of Prey, the battle is a draw.
2	SMOKE THEM OUT *Three great bonfires have been lit to burn the surrounding forest to the ground and flush out fresh prey. There are some warriors who are trying to extinguish the flames, knowing that ferocious monsters, far beyond any warband's ability to handle, will soon arrive. Thus one side seeks to keep the fires burning, while the other wishes to put them out as quickly as possible!* The players roll off, and the winner chooses who is the attacker and who is the defender. Starting with the defender, players alternate placing objectives until 3 objectives have been placed. Each objective can be placed anywhere on the battlefield more than 6" from the battlefield edge and any other objectives. At the end of each battle round, if the attacker controls an objective, it is doused – remove it from the battlefield. At the end of a battle round, if there are fewer than two objectives on the battlefield, the attacker wins. The battle ends after four battle rounds. When the battle ends, if there are two or more objectives on the battlefield, the defender wins.
3	SAVAGE TREASURES *True, this area is littered with golden treasures of incredible value, but there are also an equal number of fang-toothed horrors that will savage and maul any who come near them.* Starting with the player that won the priority roll, players alternate placing objectives until they have placed 3 objectives each. Each objective can be placed anywhere on the battlefield more than 4" from the battlefield edge and any other objectives. When a player gains control of an objective, that player rolls a dice. On 1-3, that objective is savage: allocate 3 damage points to each fighter within 3" of that objective and remove the objective from the battlefield. Otherwise the objective is now a treasure token. Once 3 treasure tokens are found, the remaining objectives are savage, and vice versa. The battle ends after four battle rounds. When the battle ends, the player with the most fighters carrying treasure tokens wins. If both players have the same number of fighters carrying treasure tokens, the battle is a draw.

4. TWIST

Roll a dice. On a 1-3, roll another dice and consult chart A to generate a twist for your battle in Thondia. On a 4-6, roll another dice and consult chart B.

D6	CHART A
1	LAIR OF THE BEASTS *This battle is fought near the lair of two great monsters. While the monsters are mostly content sleeping, if awoken, they lazily lash out at whatever is nearby before turning back over.* The player that won the priority roll picks one terrain feature, then the other player picks a different terrain feature. After a fighter ends a move action or makes an attack action within 3" of that terrain feature, roll a dice. On a 1-2, allocate 6 damage points to that fighter. If that fighter is taken down, this twist no longer applies to that terrain feature for the remainder of the battle (crunch!).
2	THE HUNTERS HUNTED *The warbands are hunted by a pack of vicious beasts that will lunge forward to pick off stragglers or any who linger too long near twitching bushes.* At the end of each battle round, roll a dice for each fighter within 6" of a battlefield edge. On a 1-2, that fighter is taken down.

3	**NEVER GO ALONE** *A pack of hidden predators lurks in the undergrowth, waiting for warriors to stray too far from their warband.* At the end of each battle round, roll a dice for the fighter that is furthest from the center of the battlefield. On a 1-5, that fighter is taken down. If more than one fighter is tied to be the furthest from the centre, the players roll off, and the winner decides which fighter is rolled for.
4	**HUNTING ANIMALS** *The attackers have launched an ambush, led to the hunt by a pack of loyal and well-trained beasts.* Before the first activation in the first battle round, each fighter in the warband of the player who won the priority roll can make one bonus move action. Their Move characteristic is 3 for that move action.
5	**ALERTED TO DANGER** *The defenders have been warned of their attackers' approach by the howls, yips and caws of their vigilant sentinels, who sniff the area and patrol the skies to keep their masters safe.* Before the first activation in the first battle round, each fighter in the warband of the player who lost the priority roll can make one move action. Their Move characteristic is 3 for that move action.
6	**KRULE TRICKZ** *This battlefield was once a Kruleboyz camp, and the murk in which the fighters battle contains all kinds of horrid surprises.* After an activation in which a fighter was allocated 1 or more damage points, allocate 1 damage point to that fighter.

D6	CHART B
1	**CONSTRICTING VINES** *A carpet of vines cover every flat surface of the battlefield, and if one is too slow or falls, they are quickly covered from head to foot and slowly crushed into a gooey pulp that feeds the surrounding lush green flora.* After a fighter's activation, if that fighter did not make a move action, or if that fighter fell, allocate 1 damage point to that fighter.
2	**TRIBAL SPIRITS** *A tribe once lived on this battlefield. Perhaps they were massacred by the forces of Order who needed their land, or were simply eaten by a rampaging monster. Either way, their angry spirits haunt these ruins and inflict a great madness on those who battle nearby.* Whilst a fighter is within 1" of a terrain feature, add 1 to the Attacks characteristic of that fighter's attack actions that have a Range characteristic of 3 or less that target an enemy fighter within 1" of the attacker.
3	**BLOOD IN THE AIR** *As fighters suffer wounds, the blood that fills the air makes them a tempting target for more feral or vicious fighters.* Add 1 to the Attacks characteristic of attack actions that have a Range characteristic of 3 or less that target an enemy fighter that has any damage points allocated to them.
4	**FEEDING FRENZY** *The feral instincts of Ghur overwhelm all, replacing reason and sense with a deep and endless hunger for raw flesh.* After resolving an attack action that allocated 1 or more damage to an enemy fighter, remove 1 damage point allocated to each friendly fighter within 1" of that enemy fighter. Each time an enemy fighter is taken down within 1" of a friendly fighter, roll dice for each friendly fighter within 1" of that fighter. Remove a number of damage points from that fighter equal to the roll.
5	**STRUGGLE FOR DOMINANCE** *As fighters are taken down, those who deal the final blow find their predatory instincts honed to a razor's edge, but all who look upon them see a rival alpha, who must be taken down to assert dominance over the others.* If there is no Alpha on the battlefield, after a fighter's attack action takes down an enemy fighter, that fighter becomes the Alpha. Add 1 to the damage points allocated to enemy fighters by each hit and critical hit from attack actions made by the Alpha. In addition, add 1 to the Attacks characteristic of attack actions that target the Alpha. Each time the damage from a fighter's attack action takes down the Alpha, that fighter becomes the Alpha.
6	**PLANNED TO PERFECTION** *One leader has pulled off the perfect ambush and has lured the enemy into a battleground of their choosing.* The players roll off. The winner chooses one twist from either chart A or chart B to apply for this battle.

RICHES OF THONDIA

If you have just played a battle in Thondia and are searching for a lesser artefact, you can use the following method instead of the usual one.

Roll a dice. On a 1-3, roll another dice and consult chart A to generate a lesser artefact from your battle in Thondia. On a 4-6, roll another dice and consult chart B.

D6	CHART A
1	**SAVAGE AXE** *Studded with the teeth of a thousand times a thousand slain prey, this axe chews through bone with ease.* [Perishable]: Once per battle, after the bearer makes an attack action, change one hit from that attack action to a critical hit.
2	**HUNTER'S PRIDE** *This amulet represents the pride of the whole warband and spurs the bearer forward to prove themselves in the eyes of their peers.* [Perishable]: Once per battle, before the bearer makes a move action, add 2 to the move characteristic of the bearer until the end of the battle round. However, they much finish each move action they make in that battle round at least as close to the enemy fighter that was nearest to them at the start of the move action.
3	**PRIMAL HORN** *A blast on this horn instils great courage in those nearby.* [Perishable]: Once per battle, when the bearer is activated, they can use this artefact. If they do, the bearer has the (☀) until the end of the battle round.
4	**EYE OF THE PREDATOR** *As long as it remains mounted in a helm or on the bearer's forehead, few weak points can escape this hunter's eye.* [Perishable]: Once per battle, before the bearer makes an attack action, they can use this artefact. If they do, subtract 1 from the Toughness characteristic (to a minimum of 1) of the target fighter until the end of the battle round.
5	**CHARM OF THE LAIZARD** *Torn from the socket of the beast itself, those who carry this pulsing eye can cause it to shoot a great beam of Ghurish energy before it dissolves into grimy pulp.* [Consumable]: The bearer can use this lesser artefact as a bonus action. If they do, draw a line 1" wide between them and a visible enemy fighter within 6". Allocate 2 damage points to each fighter touched by that line, excluding the bearer.
6	**TOTEM OF THE WILD** *With a swift prayer and howl of glee, the bearer becomes as savage and animalistic as those they hunt.* [Perishable]: Once per battle, when the bearer is activated, the bearer can choose to activate this artefact. If they do, the bearer has the (🐾) until the end of the battle round.

D6	CHART A
1	**SPEAR OF THE RUINBEAST** *This spear can be thrown great distances by a skilled fighter or used to stab an enemy that is just out of reach.* [Perishable]: Once per battle, before the bearer makes an attack action, add 2 to the Range characteristic of that attack action.
2	**BLUE-RINGED SCOIL VENOM SAC** *By devouring this venom sac whole, the vile contents force the user to regurgitate violently and explosively over nearby foes, the projected contents of their stomach now coated in virulent, poison. However, while the venom sac often and mysteriously grants an immunity to the lethal substances contained within to the imbiber, it is by no means a guarantee ...* [Consumable]: The bearer can use this lesser artefact as a bonus action. If they do, roll a dice. On a 1, allocate 3 damage points to the bearer. On a 2-4, allocate 2 damage points to a visible enemy fighter within 6" of the bearer. On a 5+, allocate 3 damage points to a visible enemy fighter within 6" of the bearer.
3	**BLOOD OF THE VIGORLAN** *The vigorlan is one of the most cunning beasts in all of Thondia. Fierce, quick-witted, and with lightning-fast reactions, painting its blood on your face is said to grant fleeting visions of the future, but only while you are being hunted.* [Perishable]: Each time an ability is used by an enemy fighter within 6" of the bearer, roll a dice. On a 4+, the player controlling the bearer gains an additional wild dice in the hero phase of the next battle round. Only one additional wild dice can be gained in this way per battle round.

4	**MARK OF THONDIA** *Vigorous, bold and of bloody deeds are those marked by Thondia.* [Perishable]: After the second time an attack action made by the bearer takes down an enemy fighter in this battle, the bearer can make a bonus move action or a bonus attack action.
5	**SAVAGE HELM** *This great, horned helm holds within it the ferocity of cornered prey, and it enables the bearer to dodge what would certainly be deathly blows with ease.* [Perishable]: Once per battle, after the bearer is picked as the target of an attack action, change one critical hit from that attack action to a hit.
6	**THE SPLINTERED HORN OF GHUR** *When attached to a helm, this shard of horn gives the wearer fierce momentum and imbues them with terrible strength. However, if they remain still, the horn saps their life energy, thus forcing them to sprint at full tilt for as long as they wear it.* [Perishable]: After the bearer makes a move action, until the end of that activation, add 2 to the Strength characteristic of this fighter's attack actions with a Range characteristic of 3 or less. When the bearer makes an attack action that has a Range characteristic of 3 or less in an activation in which they did not make a move action, subtract 2 from the Strength characteristic of that attack action (to a minimum of 1).

WARCHIEFS OF THONDIA

For anyone to survive more than a day in Thondia, uncommon strength of body, character and will is a must. Those who overcome the trials of daily life in that realm are formidable foes indeed.

If you have just played a battle in Thondia and are generating a command trait, you can choose from those listed below.

COMMAND TRAIT
CAGEY PREY *Few fighters can stall this powerful hunter's stride.* After this fighter makes a disengage action, they can immediately make a bonus move action.
UNFEELING FRENZY *This fighter is a caged animal who, when unleashed, disregards even the most heinous of wounds.* After an activation in which this fighter was allocated 1 or more damage points, remove 1 damage point allocated to this fighter.
TERRITORIAL ANGER *This fighter snarls ferally at all who would approach their downed prey or claimed lair.* This fighter counts as one additional fighter for the purposes gaining control of objectives.
POUNCING STALKER *This fighter waits for the right moment to strike before hurling themselves off a nearby high point to fall on their prey at exactly the right moment.* If this fighter falls, until the end of their activation, add 2 to the Strength characteristic of this fighter's attack actions that have a Range characteristic of 3 or less.
PACK ANIMAL *Should one of this fighter's companions fall, nothing can prevent them from exacting swift and bloody vengeance.* Each time a visible friendly fighter within 6" of this fighter is taken down, this fighter can make a bonus move action or a bonus disengage action.
GARGANT CRUSHER *'The bigger they are, the harder I hit them' is this fighter's credo.* Add 2 to the Strength characteristic of this fighter's attack actions that have a Range characteristic of 3 or less and that target a fighter that has a Wounds characteristic greater than this fighter's.

AFTERMATH

So there you have it – a guide on taking your adventures to Thondia within the realm of Ghur for a particularly savage and wild addition to your games of Warcry. We hope you enjoy your games of Warcry in this dark and dangerous realm and that you find the prey you seek!

It will come as no surprise that we would love to hear more about how your games of Warcry went, not just in Thondia but all over the Mortal Realms! As ever, do write in to team@whitedwarf.co.uk if you have any suggestions or something in particular that you'd like to read about. We may not be able to reply directly, but you might see your suggestion or question in a future issue.

DEATH AND ZEAL
Turn the page to see Vanguard Tactics' Stephen Box vs. Tabletop Tactics' Lawrence Baker in a Battle Report of top tournament players!

INDEX XENOS
Craftworld Altansar is the focus of this issue's Index Xenos. Learn of the craftworld's near-demise and their morbid hero, Maugan Ra, on page 98.

DEATH AND ZEAL

This issue's Battle Report pitches two well-known players from the tournament scene against each other. Tabletop Tactics' Lawrence Baker will be taking on Vanguard Tactics' Stephen Box in a matched play clash that pits the Drukhari against the Adepta Sororitas.

H old on to your Stratagems, kids, because this is going to be one seriously exciting Warhammer 40,000 Battle Report! This issue, two of the big names in competitive gaming have descended upon the *White Dwarf* bunker to do mighty battle against each other in a matched play game that will tickle your tactical taste buds and have you checking your Codexes for rules you never knew you had.

Commanding the Adepta Sororitas from the Order of the Bloody Rose is Stephen Box. A veteran hobbyist of many years, Stephen runs Vanguard Tactics, a website dedicated

to teaching people how to play Warhammer 40,000 and getting the most out of their armies. Opposing him is Lawrence Baker and his Drukhari force. Another long-time hobbyist, Lawrence runs Tabletop Tactics – a YouTube channel that focuses on rules commentary and Battle Reports. Both players have impressive gaming records, having competed in Warhammer 40,000 tournaments and events, both in the UK and abroad. So who better to play one of the new missions from the War Zone Nachmund: Grand Tournament mission pack? Prepare yourselves for a tense, action-packed, highly tactical battle from two masters of their craft. Battle awaits!

LAWRENCE BAKER
Lawrence got into the hobby when he was nine. He started playing when the Warhammer 40,000 second edition boxed set came out. He enjoys fielding fast and aggressive armies, getting into combat where possible and overwhelming his opponent with a 'death by a thousand cuts'. Lawrence has a fondness for Grey Knights, Emperor's Children, World Eaters and Flesh Tearers, but his all-time favourite army is Drukhari, and he is currently using them at events. His previous accolades include being the winner of Warhammer World's Grand Tournament Heat 1, Best Drukhari player in the ITC and four-time champion of No Retreat (run by SN Battle Reports). Lawrence currently runs a YouTube channel and a website, both called Tabletop Tactics, which specialise in producing entertaining Battle Reports covering everything from narrative to competitive play.

STEPHEN BOX
Stephen first got into the hobby when he was thirteen, but he didn't get into it seriously until almost two decades later. His favourite armies are anything fast and combat based, such as Harlequins, Blood Angels, Craftworld Aeldari and Adepta Sororitas. He also enjoys fielding fragile armies because he knows that if he makes a mistake he will be punished for it; for Stephen, that's a great learning opportunity! Since being back in the hobby, he's won or achieved podium positions in many Grand Tournaments and independent competitions. Last year, he won Best in Faction for Blood Angels in the International Tournament Circuit global rankings. He currently runs Vanguard Tactics, a site that aims to teach people to become great decision makers and to develop their skills to think critically while remaining composed and confident in their ability to play Warhammer 40,000.

GRAND TOURNAMENT GAMES IN WAR ZONE NACHMUND
As with all games of Warhammer, there were a few stages that took place before the Battle Report kicked off. Lawrence and Stephen guide us through the pre-game sequence.

1. SELECT BATTLE SIZE
Stephen: Seeing as most events and tournaments are fought at Strike Force size, we've decided it makes sense to show off the Nachmund rules in a 2,000-point game.

2. MUSTER ARMIES
Lawrence: If you're playing competitively, especially with people you don't know, we recommend having a chat with them about your armies before the game. It's good etiquette to have that conversation, as it is an opportunity to make sure you both know what you're up against. Stephen, do you mind me asking you about your army?

Stephen: Not at all, Lawrence. What questions do you have for me?

Lawrence: I see you are using Sisters of Battle. Are they from the Order of the Bloody Rose? They are? Great – that's +1 Attack and -1 AP to their attacks when they charge, right?

Stephen: And if they are charged, too.

Lawrence: I didn't know that! Do you have any Stratagems or abilities that enable them to advance and charge, or abilities that allow them to shoot or fight twice?

Stephen: Morvenn Vahl can fight twice once per game. The Canoness can advance and charge. She also has the Word of the Emperor Blessing, which means she can make a unit fight last if they are within 3" of her. Once per battle, she can also negate a unit's invulnerable save for a turn.

Lawrence: Now that's very important information to know. My Archon can also make an enemy unit fight last, but I wouldn't want him losing his 2+ invulnerable save. I think he'll try to avoid her! Do you have any questions about my force?

Stephen: I do. Are you using Kabal of the Black Heart?

Lawrence: I am. Each time they shoot or fight, I can re-roll one hit roll. I also count Power from Pain as one turn higher.

Stephen: So you can advance and charge with your whole army from the first turn – nasty! Oh, except the Incubi and Scourges because they're not part of the Kabal, right? And I see a lot of heavy weapons. What have you got in your units?

Lawrence: There's fifteen dark lances across the nine vehicles, plus a blaster in each Kabalite Warrior unit and four shredders in each squad of Scourges.

3. DETERMINE MISSION
Stephen: We've looked at the new missions in the War Zone Nachmund mission pack and decided to play Death and Zeal (page 52). You need to get stuck in with this mission, and it doesn't reward cagey playing, so there will be plenty of action taking place. It will provide for a more exciting spectacle, both for the Battle Report and for us as players. Also, the mission name is very fitting for the armies we picked!

4. READ MISSION BRIEFING
Lawrence: Always have a good read of the mission before you start as there may be rules you haven't encountered before that are key to victory. In this case, we noticed the Objective Purged rule, which means that units with the Objective Secured ability can move in, claim them, then move away while still leaving the objective under your control. I like this rule – it's a great way to show the importance of fielding Troops units in a balanced army.

The pre-game sequence continues on page 68 after Lawrence and Stephen talk about their army lists.

DRUKHARI – KABAL OF THE VOID SPIDER

Lawrence: My army list for this Battle Report is somewhat experimental. It's a spin-off of a relatively successful Kabal and Wych Cult army list I've been using recently. However, this time I have decided to replace the Wych Cult Patrol that I was fielding with three units of Scourges and three Ravagers! Recently on the tournament scene, Adeptus Mechanicus armies have been running riot with their Iron Striders and twenty-man phalanx hordes. We are also seeing the great Waaagh! emerge in the form of Ork Speed Freek lists featuring anywhere up to fifteen-plus vehicles!

As a result, I wanted to try a list that could really maximise the anti-tank potential Drukhari can bring whilst also covering a weakness that I have with massed infantry. This would be put to the extra test as I knew that I would be facing Stephen's infantry-based Adepta Sororitas, so a real trial by fire for my new list!

THE SPIDER!

No list of mine would be complete without 'the Spider' himself. The long-serving Archon of 'the Void Spiders' will be leading my army into battle. I have also given him the Ancient Evil Warlord Trait so that I can force an enemy unit to fight last in combat (an ability that has literally won me games against tough combat armies in the past). I'll be using the rules for the Kabal of the Black Heart, making my dark lances very efficient (I get a re-roll to hit for every unit).

GETTING TO THE POINT
This game was played back in September 2021. Although we have used the War Zone Nachmund: Grand Tournament mission pack in the Battle Report, some of the points values may have subsequently changed. However, all points were correct at the time the battle was fought.

HOW MANY DARK LANCES?

With six dark lances on my Raiders and a further nine on my Ravagers, I should be able to blow most vehicle-heavy armies off the board. I can also support this firepower with six more blasters in my units of Kabalite Warriors. These small units are very useful at performing secondary objective actions for me when needed. To deal with hordes, I have included three units of Scourges. Each unit has been equipped with four shredders – an ideal weapon for targeting large blobs of infantry as each gun gets D6 shots at S 6, -1 AP with the Blast special rule.

As good as the Scourges are, I can't rely on them alone to clear all the enemy infantry, so I have also included three units of Incubi and Drazhar in my force. These vicious murderers can butcher hordes or elite infantry alike with a large number of high-quality attacks. Drazhar can arguably take on most single characters in the game, with his Warlord Trait allowing him to re-roll all hit and wound rolls. I love these guys. Let's hope they perform!

INEXHAUSTIBLE HATRED

Few Aeldari harbour as much hatred for Chaos in all its guises as those of Altansar. They have seen what horrors it is capable of, and all have experienced great loss to it in one form or another.

Use this Stratagem in the Fight phase, when an **ALTANSAR** unit from your army is selected to fight. Until the end of the phase, each time a model in that unit makes a melee attack against a **DAEMON** unit (excluding **VEHICLE** and **MONSTER** units), add 1 to that attack's wound roll.

2 COMMAND POINTS

WITHERING VOLLEYS

Maugan Ra's influence has ensured that not only are Altansar's Dark Reapers amongst the finest of their kind but that all warriors of the craftworld are superlative shots. In the fierce fighting that the Altansari have engaged in for millennia, these skills have served them well time and time again.

Use this Stratagem in your Shooting phase, when an **ALTANSAR** unit from your army is selected to shoot. Until the end of the phase, each time a model in that unit makes an attack with an Aeldari missile launcher or Reaper launcher, improve the Armour Penetration characteristic of that attack by 1. If that unit has the **DARK REAPERS** keyword, this Stratagem costs 2CP; otherwise, it costs 1CP.

1/2 COMMAND POINTS

DEFIANT TO THE LAST

The hardship the Altansari have endured for so many millennia has greatly hardened their souls and their bodies. With no safe harbours to flee to in the Eye of Terror and no allies to call upon, they have learnt to hold their ground and fight to the bitter end in order to ensure their survival.

Use this Stratagem at the start of your Command phase. Select one **ALTANSAR** unit from your army. Until the start of your next Command phase, that unit gains the Objective Secured ability (see the Warhammer 40,000 Core Book).

2 COMMAND POINTS

THRICE-LAYERED WARDS

It is a wonder that, after millennia in the Eye of Terror, the Altansari appear to have escaped without being corrupted by the forces of Chaos. Though this is a mystery to a great many Aeldari, what is clear is that the grim craftworlders have hardened their minds to the influence of the warp and have layered many wards onto their armour.

Use this Stratagem in your opponent's Psychic phase, when an **ALTANSAR** unit from your army would suffer a mortal wound. Until the end of the phase, each time a model in that unit would lose a wound, roll one D6: on a 4+, that wound is not lost.

1 COMMAND POINT

FACTION TERRAIN WARSCROLL

HERDSTONE

Wrought from the Chaos-infused substance of the realms, Herdstones are the sites at which the Beasts of Chaos carry out their savage rituals. As the Greatfrays stampede further into civilised territories, they continue to erect Herdstones, from which the corruptive taint of the anarchic wilds bleeds freely into the land.

FACTION TERRAIN: Only Beasts of Chaos armies can include this faction terrain feature.

SET-UP: After territories are determined, you can set up this faction terrain feature wholly within your territory and more than 3" from all objectives and other terrain features. If both players can set up faction terrain features at the same time, they must roll off and the winner chooses who sets up their faction terrain features first.

IMPASSABLE: You cannot move a model over this terrain feature unless it can fly, and you cannot move a model onto this terrain feature or set up a model on this terrain feature (even if it can fly).

Entropic Lodestone: *As the corrupting influence of the Herdstone spreads, buildings, armour and other trappings of civilisation and order begin to crumble to dust, allowing even the crude weapons of the Beasts of Chaos to cut through their defences with ease.*

Improve the Rend characteristic of melee weapons used by all friendly **BEASTS OF CHAOS** units on the battlefield by 1. From the start of the third battle round, improve the Rend characteristic of melee weapons used by all friendly **BEASTS OF CHAOS** units on the battlefield by 2 instead of 1.

Locus of Savagery: *A Herdstone marks the domain of the Beasts of Chaos, and in its presence they fight with unfailing vigour.*

After this terrain feature is set up, its range is 12". At the start of each battle round after the first, its range is increased by 6".

If a friendly **BEASTS OF CHAOS** unit wholly within range of this terrain feature fails a battleshock test, halve the number of models that flee from that unit (rounding down). In addition, if a friendly **BEASTS OF CHAOS** unit wholly within range of this terrain feature receives the Rally command, you can return 1 slain model to that unit for each 4+ instead of each 6.

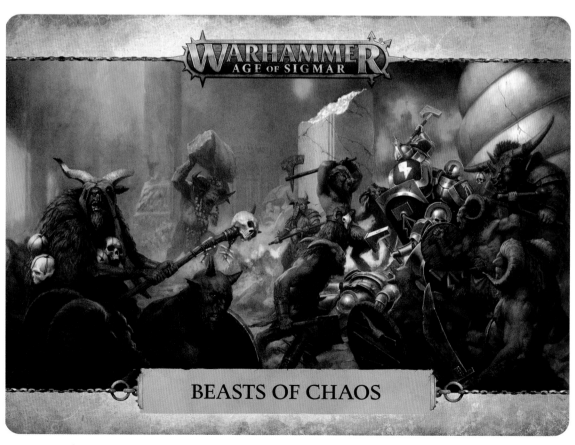

BEASTS OF CHAOS

KABAL OF THE VOID SPIDER (BLACK HEART)

Battalion Detachment

HQ

1	**Archon**	
	– Husk Blade	
	– Warlord Trait: Ancient Evil	**85 pts**
2	**Drazhar**	
	– Warlord Trait: Hatred Eternal	**145 pts**

TROOPS

3	**5 Kabalite Warriors**	**50 pts**
	– 1 blaster	
4	**5 Kabalite Warriors**	**50 pts**
	– 1 blaster	
5	**5 Kabalite Warriors**	**50 pts**
	– 1 blaster	
6	**5 Kabalite Warriors**	**50 pts**
	– 1 blaster	
7	**5 Kabalite Warriors**	**50 pts**
	– 1 blaster	
8	**5 Kabalite Warriors**	**50 pts**
	– 1 blaster	

ELITES

9	**5 Incubi**	**80 pts**
10	**5 Incubi**	**80 pts**
11	**5 Incubi**	**80 pts**

FAST ATTACK

12	**5 Scourges**	
	– 4 shredders	**80 pts**
13	**5 Scourges**	
	– 4 shredders	**80 pts**
14	**5 Scourges**	
	– 4 shredders	**80 pts**

HEAVY SUPPORT

15	**Ravager**	
	– 3 dark lances	**140 pts**
16	**Ravager**	
	– 3 dark lances	**140 pts**
17	**Ravager**	
	– 3 dark lances	**140 pts**

DEDICATED TRANSPORT

18	**Raider**	
	– 1 dark lance	**95 pts**
19	**Raider**	
	– 1 dark lance	**95 pts**
20	**Raider**	
	– 1 dark lance	**95 pts**
21	**Raider**	
	– 1 dark lance	**95 pts**
22	**Raider**	
	– 1 dark lance	**95 pts**
23	**Raider**	
	– 1 dark lance	**95 pts**

Total Points: 2000
Starting Command Points: 11
Pre-battle Stratagems: Tolerated Ambition (1CP) on the Archon
Secondary Objectives: Assassination, Engage on All Fronts, Retrieve Nachmund Data

SECONDARY OBJECTIVES

Lawrence: I chose Assassination because Stephen has a character-heavy army. When he finds out I have that secondary objective, he will have to play more cagily with his heroes or else give up valuable victory points when they get assassinated. It also feels like a very Drukhari kind of objective! Because we're deploying in table quarters, I picked Engage on All Fronts, which is relatively easy to achieve as you can hop units into adjacent quarters to score easy points early on. My third choice is Retrieve Nachmund Data. If I'm going to be moving into multiple table quarters for Engage on All Fronts, I may as well capitalise on that and score again! My small units of Kabalites are perfect for achieving this secondary objective.

END GAME OBJECTIVE

ASSASSINATION

The enemy looks to their champions for courag Identify and eliminate them with extreme prejud.

Score 3 victory points at the end of the battle f each enemy **CHARACTER** model that is destroye If the enemy **WARLORD** was destroyed during th battle, gain 1 additional victory point.

PURGE THE ENEMY

PROGRESSIVE OBJECTIVE

ENGAGE ON ALL FRONTS

No part of the battlefield can be left unchalleng

Score 2 victory points at the end of your turn you have one or more qualifying units (see belc from your army wholly within three different table quarters, and those units are all more that from the centre of the battlefield. Score 3 victo points instead if you have one or more qualifyi units from your army wholly within each tabl quarter, and those units are all more than 6" fr the centre of the battlefield. A qualifying unit one that contains 3 or more models, or one th contains 1 or more **VEHICLE** or **MONSTER** model

BATTLEFIELD SUPREMACY

END GAME OBJECTIVE

RETRIEVE NACHMUND DATA

Several servo-skulls containing vital data have been lost within this region. Locate and retrieve these at all cost.

If you select this objective, keep a Retrieved Data tally. In addition, units in your army can perform the following action:

Retrieve Data (Action): One **INFANTRY** or **BIKER** unit from your army can start to perform this action at the end of your Movement phase if it is wholly within a table quarter that has not had a servo-skull retrieved by your army (see below) and it is more than 6" away from any other table quarter. This action is completed at the end of your turn provided the unit attempting it is still within the same table quarter. If this action is successfully completed, roll one D6, subtracting 1 from the result if the unit that completed the action has the Troops battlefield role; if the result is less than or equal to the number of models currently in that unit, that table quarter is said to have had a servo-skull retrieved by your army and you add 1 to your Retrieved Data tally.

At the end of the battle, score 4 victory points if your Retrieved Data tally is 2, score 8 victory points if your tally is 3, or score 12 victory points if your tally is 4.

SHADOW OPERATIONS

ADEPTA SORORITAS – ORDER OF THE BLOODY ROSE

Stephen: I decided to pick the Adepta Sororitas for this Battle Report for a couple of reasons. Firstly, I absolutely love the new model range. Secondly, I get the most enjoyment out of the game when I am playing a fast combat army. This is something that the Adepta Sororitas do extremely well, particularly the Order of the Bloody Rose, which is why I decided to collect them and field them in this battle.

THINKING ABOUT OBJECTIVES

With regards to my army choices, I use the same method every time when writing my lists. I start by looking at the primary objective (or objectives, in the case of a tournament) and ensuring that I have enough units to control objectives in my turn, plus enough other units to kick the enemy off their objectives. This is where the Battle Sisters, Dogmata and Zephyrim really shine. My four units of Battle Sisters have the Objective Secured ability, while the Dogmata can give a Core unit the same ability until your next turn. If I play that on the Zephyrim, my potential for stealing objectives from my opponent is greatly increased. Saint Celestine fulfils a similar role. Her high movement means that she can fly out and take control of an objective if required, while her 6" Heroic Intervention makes her ideal for protecting objectives, too.

I then look at secondary objectives and make sure that in every game and mission I have good options available to

> **'Whoa, you have got some serious guns there, mate. That's a lot of cheeky firepower. We've got some obscuring terrain, yeah?' - Stephen**

me. As my army list plays to the primary objectives well, it should also be able to score Stranglehold consistently. I will often pick To the Last as a secondary objective with Celestine, Morvenn Vahl and my large unit of Sacresants being my most expensive units. The Battle Sisters who deploy in the Rhinos can also help me perform actions, such as those in the Shadow Operations category.

THE OTHER TASTY STUFF

To finish off the list, I've included several damage-dealing units in the form of the Repentia and my Canoness. They are there to counter-charge if the enemy gets too close and push them back where required. I also added two units of Retributors to the list to deal damage at range and tackle larger threats that my other units can't take on.

What I love about this list is that it's flexible enough to attack or defend, can take on most opposition armies pretty well and has plenty of tools in the tool box for some of the tougher adversaries out there.

ORDER OF THE BLOODY ROSE

Supreme Command Detachment
HQ
1 **Morvenn Vahl**
– Warlord Trait: Righteous Rage **265 pts**

Battalion Detachment
HQ
2 **Canoness**
– Blessed Blade
– Warlord Trait: Blazing Ire
– Blessing: Word of the Emperor
– Relic: Chaplet of Sacrifice **100 pts**
3 **Celestine**
– 2 Geminae Superia **200 pts**
4 **Hospitaller**
– Relic: Litanies of Faith **50 pts**

TROOPS
5 **5 Battle Sisters**
– 1 chainsword **55 pts**
6 **5 Battle Sisters**
- 1 chainsword **55 pts**
7 **5 Battle Sisters**
– 1 chainsword **55 pts**
8 **5 Battle Sisters**
– 1 chainsword **55 pts**

ELITES
9 **5 Sisters Repentia** **70 pts**
10 **5 Sisters Repentia** **70 pts**
11 **10 Celestian Sacresants**
– Anointed halberds **140 pts**
12 **5 Celestian Sacresants**
– Anointed halberds **70 pts**

13 **5 Celestian Sacresants**
– Anointed halberds **70 pts**
14 **Dogmata**
– Warlord Trait: Indomitable Belief
– Relic: The Sigil Ecclesiasticus
– Hymn: Litany of Enduring Faith
– Hymn: Verse of Holy Piety **65 pts**

FAST ATTACK
15 **5 Zephyrim** **85 pts**
16 **5 Zephyrim** **85 pts**
17 **5 Zephyrim** **85 pts**

HEAVY SUPPORT
18 **5 Retributors**
– 3 multi-meltas, heavy flamer, chainsword **130 pts**
19 **5 Retributors**
– 3 multi-meltas, heavy flamer, chainsword
– Armorium Cherub **135 pts**

DEDICATED TRANSPORT
20 **Sororitas Rhino** **80 pts**
21 **Sororitas Rhino** **80 pts**

Total Points: 2000
Starting Command Points: 8
Pre-battle Stratagems: Saint in the Making (2CP) and Open the Reliquaries (2CP) on both the Canoness and Dogmata.
Secondary Objectives: Stranglehold, Bring It Down, Investigate Signal

SECONDARY OBJECTIVES

Stephen: I've picked Bring It Down because, with the recent changes in the mission pack, each of Lawrence's nine vehicles will now reward me with 2 VP when I destroy them. I should be able to max out on this objective over the course of the game. Stranglehold is also a must for me. The primary mission is to take and hold objectives, so I may as well grab some bonus victory points with Stranglehold. I reckon I can get onto three objectives in my first turn, leaving Lawrence with two. My last pick is Investigate Signal. Again, this objective has had a slight tweak, so I thought it would be worth trying out. I need to control the centre of the board for Stranglehold, so I can potentially have one unit complete two objectives each turn.

PROGRESSIVE OBJECTIVE
STRANGLEHOLD
Maintain a stranglehold on your foe by dominating key strategic locations in the area.

Score 3 victory points at the end of your turn if you control 3 or more objective markers and you also control more objective marker than your opponent controls.

BATTLEFIELD SUPREMACY

END GAME OBJECTIVE
BRING IT DOWN
The opposing army contains numerous heavily armoured units. Take any opportunity to bring them down.

Score 1 victory point at the end of the battle for each enemy MONSTER or VEHICLE model with a Wounds characteristic of 9 or less that is destroyed, 2 victory points for each enemy MONSTER or VEHICLE model with a Wounds characteristic of between 10-14 that is destroyed and 3 victory points for each enemy MONSTER or VEHICLE model with a Wounds characteristic of or more that is destroyed.

PURGE THE ENEMY

PROGRESSIVE OBJECTIVE
INVESTIGATE SIGNAL
A mysterious signal has been received by our fleet in the Nachmund war zone, and its source has been identified as originating somewhere in the vicinity of this battlefield. You must secure, search and locate it without delay.

Score 3 victory points each time a unit from your army successfully completes the following action:

Investigate Signal (Action): One INFANTRY unit from your army that contains 3 or more models can start to perform this action at the end of your Movement phase if it is wholly within 6" of the centre of the battlefield. This action is completed at the end of your turn provided the unit attempting it is still wholly within 6" of the centre of the battlefield and no enemy units (excluding AIRCRAFT units) are wholly within 6" of the centre of the battlefield.

SHADOW OPERATIONS

PRE-GAME SEQUENCE CONTINUED

With their armies picked ready for battle and the mission read through carefully, Lawrence and Stephen take us through the rest of the pre-game sequence.

5. PLACE OBJECTIVE MARKERS

Lawrence: Five objective markers – one in each quarter and one in the centre. Nice and easy. The quartered deployment means that some of those objectives are pretty close right at the start of the game, and if I don't race out to get them, Stephen will!

6. CREATE THE BATTLEFIELD

Stephen: We're setting up the battlefield just like the tables at the US Open that took place in Orlando last year. The terrain features all have footprints, so it's easy to define their borders. It's always worth having a discussion with your opponent before the game about what rules each piece of terrain has and (if they don't have obvious footprints) where the borders of each building end and how (or even if!) line of sight can be drawn through them. In this game, the four main buildings and the two at either end have the Obscuring trait, while the four in the corners have the Dense Cover rule.

7. DETERMINE ATTACKER AND DEFENDER

Lawrence: I've won the roll-off, so, seeing as I'm the evil pain-loving Drukhari, I'll be the attacker.

8. CHOOSE DEPLOYMENT ZONE

Stephen: As Lawrence is the attacker, I get to pick the deployment zone. I'm taking the south-west corner with the large building, so I can hide most of my infantry in it!

9. SELECT SECONDARY OBJECTIVES

Stephen: You need to think about your own objectives carefully – does your opponent have enough vehicles for Bring It Down to be worthwhile? Will picking To the Last make you play too defensively with your best units? It's important to check facts, too. For example, does Celestine have to be 'dead', or 'proper dead' for the purposes of Assassination (*it's the latter* – E*d*)? You also need to try to predict what secondaries your opponent is going to pick. If you were them, which ones would you pick? Now, how can you stop them achieving them?

10. DECLARE RESERVES AND TRANSPORTS

Lawrence: Neither of us is keeping units in reserve in this battle as we both think the other will zone off sections of the board to prevent units arriving. During this stage, we also explain which units are in which vehicles. You can see our deployed forces below.

11. DEPLOY ARMIES

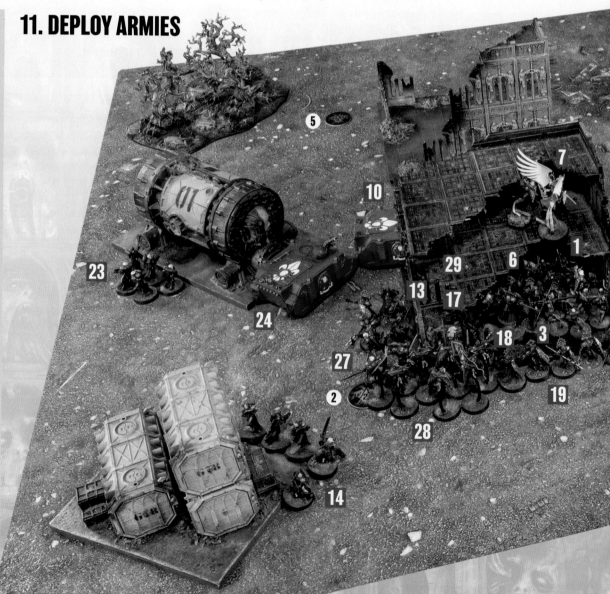

Stephen places two units of Repentia and a unit of ten Sacresants in the south-west building **(1-3)**, while Lawrence deploys an empty Raider on the eastern board edge **(4)**. He leaves five Kabalites to stand guard over objective 1 **(5)**.

The Canoness **(6)** and Saint Celestine **(7)** join the scrum in Stephen's corner as more Kabalite-filled Raiders appear to the east **(8-9)**.

Stephen places a Rhino in front of the building **(10)** with Morvenn Vahl next to it. Lawrence checks the distance to them before placing a Ravager in the north-east corner **(11)** followed by a Raider packed with Incubi and Kabalites **(12)**, who could potentially pull off a first-turn charge.

Stephen places a squad of five Sacresants **(13)** with a unit of Battle

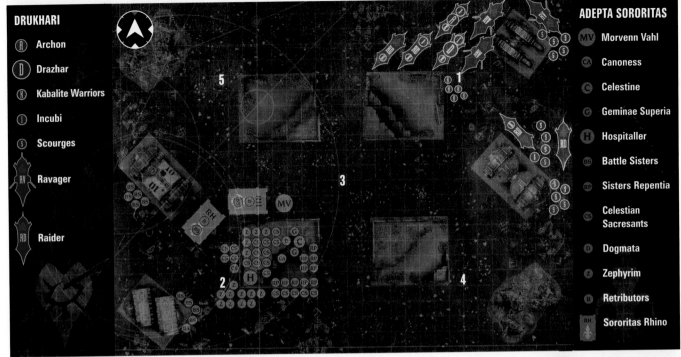

DRUKHARI

- (R) Archon
- (D) Drazhar
- (K) Kabalite Warriors
- (I) Incubi
- (S) Scourges
- (RV) Ravager
- (RD) Raider

ADEPTA SORORITAS

- (MV) Morvenn Vahl
- (CA) Canoness
- (C) Celestine
- (G) Geminae Superia
- (H) Hospitaller
- (BS) Battle Sisters
- (RP) Sisters Repentia
- (CS) Celestian Sacresants
- (D) Dogmata
- (Z) Zephyrim
- (R) Retributors
- (RH) Sororitas Rhino

Sisters nearby (14) to claim objective 2. Lawrence responds by placing two units of Scourges in cover (15-16). Again, he checks ranges to see how far they can potentially move and shoot.

The Hospitaller (17) and Dogmata (18) deploy inside the building with a unit of Sacresants just outside (19).

Two more Ravagers (20-21) and a third unit of Scourges (22) appear in the north-east corner.

Stephen places a unit of Battle Sisters behind the generator (23). He places his second Rhino nearby (24). Like the first, it contains a unit of Battle Sisters and a unit of Retributors.

Lawrence places the Raiders containing his Archon (25), Drazhar (26) and their attending retinues of Incubi and Kabalites.

Stephen deploys his three units of Zephyrim either in or around his new command building (27-29).

TOP TIP!

Stephen: If you've got transport vehicles in your army, check distances around them. Can the units inside disembark and reach objectives? Can other units then embark so they are protected from enemy fire? If the vehicle is destroyed, where will the units inside go? While deploying, I left an empty space in the corner of the building in my deployment zone for just that reason. If my Rhino is destroyed in the first turn, I can disembark my Retributors 3" into that gap and stop Lawrence from shooting them.

BATTLE ROUND 1: CAGEY FIRST MOVES

In which both players try to outflank each other while simultaneously keeping the bulk of their armies at a safe distance. Few shots are fired, but casualties are still taken.

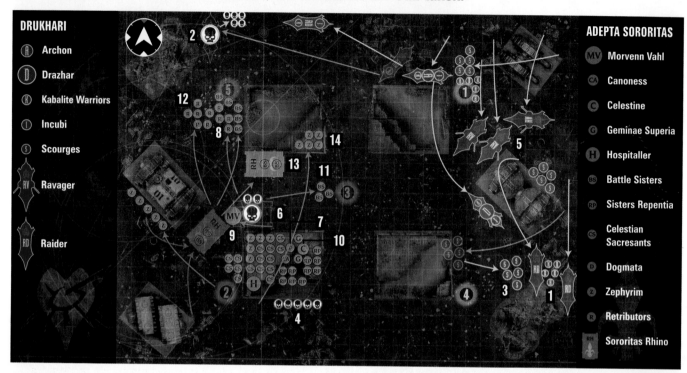

DRUKHARI
- (A) Archon
- (D) Drazhar
- (K) Kabalite Warriors
- (I) Incubi
- (S) Scourges
- (RV) Ravager
- (RD) Raider

ADEPTA SORORITAS
- (MV) Morvenn Vahl
- (CA) Canoness
- (C) Celestine
- (G) Geminae Superia
- (H) Hospitaller
- (BS) Battle Sisters
- (RP) Sisters Repentia
- (CS) Celestian Sacresants
- (D) Dogmata
- (Z) Zephyrim
- (R) Retributors
- (RH) Sororitas Rhino

TURN 1: LAWRENCE

Having taken the first turn, Lawrence sets about enacting his battle plan. He starts by disembarking a unit of Kabalites and moving them into the south-west table quarter to perform the Retrieve Data action (1). He also sends two Raiders west along the north board edge, using the Enhanced Aethersails Stratagem on one of them to get within 3" of objective 5 (2).

'I'm going to move my Ravagers about to draw line of sight to some tasty targets and also to account for Stephen's deployment,' says Lawrence. 'A few of them are in charge range of Celestine, which is a bit dangerous. Even a 12" charge is a risk I want to avoid.' Lawrence also moves the Kabalites on objective 1 back slightly to stay out of Celestine's range but flies a unit of Scourges south (3) to try to draw a bead on the Sacresants in Stephen's deployment zone (4). He moves the rest of his units around the fringes of the board. 'I'm keeping the Raiders with units in them just close enough to the centre of the board so they can charge anything that tries to take the objective,' he adds. 'Stephen will want to take that objective and score the Investigate Signal objective. I want to make him hesitate about trying to complete his own objectives.'

In his Shooting phase, Lawrence's Scourges deal with a unit of Sacresants (see **Sneaky Salvo**, opposite) while the Ravagers (5) target Stephen's Rhino (6). Stephen plays the Holy Smokescreen Stratagem, enabling him to fire the vehicle's

> 'It's good practice to explain your intent to your opponent. By showing Stephen I'm within 3" of an objective, there's no chance for ambiguity later.' - Lawrence

smoke launchers. They prevent a few shots finding their target, but Lawrence is still easily able to destroy the Rhino and cause a further four wounds on the Rhino behind it. Two Battle Sisters are slain disembarking from the wrecked vehicle (see **Tactical Disembarkation**, left).

TURN 2: STEPHEN

Stephen begins his turn by using his Dogmata's abilities (**7**). He plays Unflinching Determination on the disembarked Retributors (**8**), giving them the Objective Secured ability. He also plays Litany of Enduring Faith on them to improve their invulnerable save and War Hymn to give them +1 Attack. Finally, he uses Morvenn Vahl's (**9**) Commander of the Adepta Sororitas ability to give the Retributors re-rolls to hit and wound!

'I could charge Celestine (**10**) into the Scourges, but that will leave her too far from the central objective and potentially vulnerable,' says Stephen, who instead moves his unit of three Battle Sisters into the centre of the board to perform the Investigate Signal action (**11**). 'Because of the Objective Purged mission rule, I will still hold that central objective even if those Battle Sisters die,' adds Stephen. 'So Lawrence will have to move in and claim it.' He moves the Retributors onto objective 5 (**12**), along with a second unit of Retributors and a unit of Battle Sisters that disembark from the second Rhino.

The Battle Sisters who were on his western flank embark in the now-empty Rhino, which Stephen also moves north (**13**). A unit of Zephyrim join them in the assault on the north-west corner of the board (**14**). 'If I can hold the objective in my quarter, the central objective and the north one, I will be able to score maximum points from Take and Hold while simultaneously swinging around Lawrence's flank,' explains Stephen.

Stephen's Shooting phase is brief but violent. Morvenn Vahl half destroys the Raider on objective 5, which the Retributors easily finish off. Lawrence deploys the Kabalites who disembark as far from the Battle Sisters as possible to ensure their survival, but they are wiped out by the second unit of Retributors. At the end of the round, three objectives belong to Stephen, while the other two are under Lawrence's control.

SNEAKY SALVO

Having entered the building in the south-east corner, the Scourges line up their shredders on the Sacresants hiding behind the south-west building in Stephen's deployment zone. Only the two in the building can fire, but they still kill three of the elite warriors! Lawrence then uses the Never Stationary Stratagem to fly them back towards the nearby Raiders and away from a potentially vengeful Celestine. The two Raiders fire their dark lances and kill the last two Sacresants in what Lawrence describes as an 'unexpectedly efficient round of shooting.'

TACTICAL DISEMBARKATION

Having lost his lead Rhino to enemy fire, Stephen disembarks the Battle Sisters and Retributors inside. He loses two models in the vehicle's destruction and chooses to take off two of the regular Battle Sisters. This leaves him with a full squad of five Retributors, which he disembarks 3" towards objective 5, declaring 'every inch counts right now!' He disembarks the three Battle Sisters towards the centre of the table, where they will be just numerous enough (3 + models) to score the Investigate Signal objective in his own turn.

BATTLE ROUND 1 VICTORY POINTS

 4   **11**

Primary Objectives:
- 2 VP: Direct Assault

Secondary Objectives:
- 2 VP: Engage on All Fronts

Primary Objectives:
- 3 VP: Direct Assault

Secondary Objectives:
- 3 VP: Stranglehold
- 3 VP: Investigate Signal
- 2 VP: Bring It Down

BATTLE ROUND 2: DATA RETRIEVED, SIGNAL INVESTIGATED

In which secondary objectives are scored, primary objectives are attempted and the north-west corner of the battlefield turns into a bloodbath.

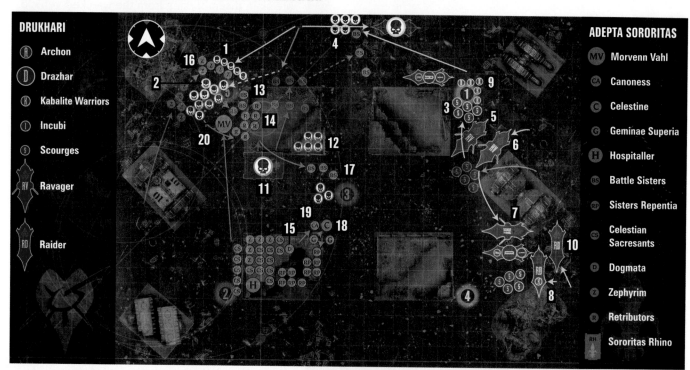

DRUKHARI

- (A) Archon
- (D) Drazhar
- (K) Kabalite Warriors
- (I) Incubi
- (S) Scourges
- (RV) Ravager
- (RD) Raider

ADEPTA SORORITAS

- (MV) Morvenn Vahl
- (CA) Canoness
- (C) Celestine
- (G) Geminae Superia
- (H) Hospitaller
- (BS) Battle Sisters
- (RP) Sisters Repentia
- (CS) Celestian Sacresants
- (D) Dogmata
- (Z) Zephyrim
- (R) Retributors
- (RH) Sororitas Rhino

TURN 1: LAWRENCE

'Stephen scored a lot of points in that first round, so now I need to strike back and prevent him scoring more,' says Lawrence. 'First, those Sisters on objective 5 need to go – they're an annoyance!' Lawrence begins his turn by moving the nearby Kabalite Warriors (1) towards the huddle of Battle Sisters. He reinforces them with a unit of Incubi (2) that disembark from a nearby transport (see **Careful Manoeuvring**, right).

The rest of Lawrence's movement is, as Stephen describes it, 'a bit cagey', with most of the Raiders hanging back while the Scourges (3-4) move out to strike and the Ravagers line up shots (5-7). 'I'm not willing to commit just yet,' explains Lawrence. 'Stephen is still holding a lot of units back, only sending out what he needs to. If I go in all guns blazing to take objectives, he will easily win. I need to be patient for another turn at least.' He also embarks one unit of Kabalites on their Raider (8), while those in his deployment zone (9) perform Retrieve Data, securing Lawrence 4 VP for the Retrieve Nachmund Data secondary objective.

Lawrence's Shooting phase starts well – a single dark lance shot from a Raider (10) obliterates Stephen's second Rhino (11), but Stephen uses Emergency Disembarkation to move the Battle Sisters who climb out of the wreckage (the six who survive, that is!) up to 6", thereby joining the fight around objective 5. The Drukhari rain of fire continues with a unit of Scourges wiping out the Battle Sisters holding the central objective before

CAREFUL MANOEUVRING

If a unit cannot be seen when it declares a charge, it cannot be shot in overwatch, which is exactly why Lawrence moves his Incubi behind, but not into, the ruined building. However, when Lawrence destroys Stephen's second Rhino, Stephen disembarks his Battle Sisters right into the intended path of the Incubi, forcing them to charge the leading (and buffed up) Retributors.

22

**DISENGAGE ...
THEN ENGAGE!**
Stephen decides to
Fall Back with his
Battle Sisters and
Retributors so that his
other units can shoot
the Incubi. Normally
units that Fall Back
can't shoot, but
Stephen uses
Judgement of the
Faithful to ensure the
Retributor can still fire.
Most armies have a
Stratagem, army rule,
order, or ability that
enables a unit to do
this. It's worth finding
out how you can use
this valuable ability in
your own battle plans.

once again flying back behind cover. The
Scourges on the north edge of the battlefield
perform similarly well, killing three of the
Zephyrim (12) in the north-east building. They
are finished off by the nearby Kabalites.

The Charge phase sees the Incubi charge the
Battle Sisters (13) and Retributors (14) holding
the objective. Lawrence reasons that, if he kills all
the models with Objective Secured, his Kabalites
can claim the objective. The Incubi slay two Battle
Sisters and three Retributors, though Stephen
saves one with the Moment of Grace Stratagem.
The Adepta Sororitas fight back and Lawrence
chooses to remove the Klaivex rather than two
Incubi to minimise losses. It's a prudent move, as
he claims the objective by a single model.

TURN 2: STEPHEN

Stephen begins his turn by using the Dogmata's
(15) many abilities. He plays Unflinching
Determination, Litany of Enduring Faith and War
Hymn on the nearby Zephyrim (16), who then fly
north towards objective 5. Morvenn Vahl uses her
Commander of the Adepta Sororitas ability to
give the unengaged Retributors re-rolls to hit and
wound, while the other Retributors and Battle
Sisters fall back from their fight with the Incubi.
Stephen uses the Judgement of the Faithful
Statagem to ensure the retreating Retributors can
still shoot. Meanwhile, three more Battle Sisters
move towards the centre of the board to
complete the Investigate Signal objective (17).
Saint Celestine (18) and the Canoness (19) move
out of the building to join them as Morvenn Vahl
heads north to help protect objective 5 (20).

Stephen's Shooting phase is surprisingly brief.
After a flurry of poor shooting from Morvenn Vahl
and the Zephyrim, the Retributors casually wipe
out the Incubi and a Raider while the rest of the
Battle Sisters in the north-west corner target the
closest unit of Scourges, killing all but one of

21

them. 'I'm not going to shoot the Kabalites,'
explains Stephen, 'as I can charge them instead
and move even more units onto the objective.' In
the Fight phase the buffed-up Zephyrim easily
kill the five Kabalite. Stephen also charges one of
his units of Battle Sisters inTo the Last surviving
Scourge. 'This is a great opportunity to block
Lawrence's movement,' says Stephen as he
strings his unit out. 'He can fly over them, but
can't move his infantry through them.' The Sisters
kill the last Scourge then hold their ground.

TOP TIP!
Stephen: Blocking
the movement of
enemy units is a
key tactic in this
game. One of the
easiest ways to do
this – and a tactic I
employed this turn
– is to string out a
unit of infantry so
they are at their
maximum 2" unit
coherency. Enemy
units can't move
between your
models, so they
will have to move
around them or
over them, if they
can fly. This is a
useful tactic if you
need to block off a
section of the
battlefield or keep
an enemy away
from an objective.
If only Raiders
didn't fly ...

BATTLE ROUND 2 VICTORY POINTS

21   **26**

Primary Objectives:
- 8 VP: Take and Hold
- 3 VP: Direct Assault

Secondary Objectives:
- 2 VP: Engage on All Fronts
- 4 VP: Retrieve Nachmund
  Data

Primary Objectives:
- 4 VP: Take and Hold
- 3 VP: Direct Assault

Secondary Objectives:
- 3 VP: Stranglehold
- 3 VP: Investigate Signal
- 2 VP: Bring It Down

BATTLE ROUND 3: A CLASH OF COMMANDERS

In which the Drukhari spring their trap and attempt to corner the Sisters of Battle. Meanwhile, the Spider pounces on the unsuspecting Morvenn Vahl.

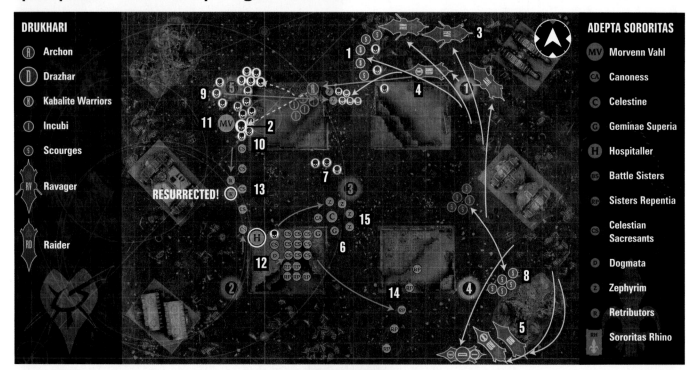

DRUKHARI

- (R) Archon
- (D) Drazhar
- (K) Kabalite Warriors
- (I) Incubi
- (S) Scourges
- (RV) Ravager
- (RD) Raider

ADEPTA SORORITAS

- (MV) Morvenn Vahl
- (CA) Canoness
- (C) Celestine
- (G) Geminae Superia
- (H) Hospitaller
- (BS) Battle Sisters
- (RP) Sisters Repentia
- (CS) Celestian Sacresants
- (D) Dogmata
- (Z) Zephyrim
- (R) Retributors
- (RH) Sororitas Rhino

RESURRECTED!

TURN 1: LAWRENCE

Lawrence flies his Scourges over the Battle Sisters trying to cordon off the battlefield (1). The high movement of the Drukhari, plus the fact they can advance and charge due to Power from Pain, also allows Lawrence to sneak a unit of Kabalites, the Incubi and his Archon past them (2). Two Ravagers join the advance along the northern board edge (3) as the Kabalites that were on objective 1 leap into the Archon's recently vacated Raider ready to move to a new location in the following turn (4). On the opposite side of the board, Lawrence moves his Raiders to harry Stephen's flank (5).

TOP TIP!

Lawrence: Before the battle, pick a few Stratagems that you would like to use rather than considering all of them. If you have five or six key Stratagems in mind, you will be able to tailor your tactics around them rather than trying to find a Stratagem to get you out of trouble.

'Saint Celestine has a 6" Heroic Intervention, yeah?' asks Lawrence, to which Stephen replies: 'That's why she's 3" from the central objective – so she can reach any Drukhari who get too close.' Lawrence decides to stay away from Celestine (6), but he shoots the three Battle Sisters nearby (7) with the Scourges (8) before flying them into the trees using Never Stationary. The rest of the Drukhari target the Battle Sisters to the north, wiping out the unit that Stephen had tried to place in their way. The Scourges eliminate three of the Zephyrim (9) hovering near the north-west building while the Ravagers target the Retributors

74

(10). One unit is destroyed, while the other is reduced to just one Battle Sister, as both Ravagers score three kills each with their dark lances.

The Charge phase sees the Kabalites fail to charge the Zephyrim, while the Incubi roll a double 1 for their charge. Lawrence uses a Command Re-roll and scores 11, enabling the Drukhari elite to avoid charging in near Morvenn Vahl (11). 'I'm going to block Vahl with my Archon,' explains Lawrence. 'He should cause some damage while stopping her from intervening with the Incubi.' The Combat phase begins as expected, with the Incubi dicing the Battle Sisters. Lawrence's Archon causes two wounds on Morvenn Vahl, who retaliates and uses her more numerous sweeping blow attacks in the hope of shorting out his Shadow Field. Lawrence gingerly rolls his saving throws one at a time. The Shadow Field collapses. The Spider dies.

TURN 2: STEPHEN

'I have a difficult choice now,' says Stephen. 'Lawrence has moved his vehicles close enough for me to reach them. I can score big on Bring It Down. But, if I do that, my characters will be in the open and he'll retaliate to score Assassination. It's a big risk-reward situation.' Stephen ultimately decides on caution and uses the Dogmata's (12) Unflinching Determination on the nearby Sacresants (13), who stand near objective 2 but also string out to protect Morvenn Vahl. The Zephyrim to the north fly towards the Kabalites hiding in the alleyway, while to the south the Repentia (14) race out to block the encroaching Raiders (see **Area Denial**, left). The other Zephyrim leap out to surround Saint Celestine (15). Stephen moves the last surviving Retributor back towards his deployment zone where he uses the Rites of Restoration Stratagem on his Hospitaller to bring one of the squad back to life. Lawrence immediately plays the Agents of Vect Stratagem, making Rites of Restoration cost 2CP every time Stephen uses it from now on.

Stephen's Shooting is minimal but effective. Morvenn Vahl and the Retributors wipe out the Incubi around objective 5, while Celestine and the Zephyrim in the centre of the board slay most of the Kabalites to the north of objective 3. The unit of two Zephyrim charge the Kabalites and kill the last two Drukhari in the Fight phase.

AREA DENIAL

With the Drukhari able to move, advance and charge, Stephen's power base in the south-west corner comes under threat from the encroaching Raiders (one of which contains Drazhar and a unit of Incubi). To stop them leaping out of their vehicles and charging into the building, Stephen uses a Miracle dice to advance a unit of Repentia as far as possible and string them out to block the Drukhari. The Raiders could easily move over them, but then the units inside would not be able to disembark and charge – a tricky dilemma for Lawrence.

'Perhaps, in hindsight, I should have picked To the Last, as my most expensive units are all still alive. It's one of the objectives my army is built around.' - Stephen

BATTLE ROUND 3 VICTORY POINTS

34   **43**

Primary Objectives:
- 8 VP: Take and Hold
- 3 VP: Direct Assault

Secondary Objectives:
- 2 VP: Engage on All Fronts

Primary Objectives:
- 8 VP: Take and Hold
- 3 VP: Direct Assault

Secondary Objectives:
- 3 VP: Stranglehold
- 3 VP: Investigate Signal

BATTLE ROUND 4: SLAY THE WARLORD

Wherein the Drukhari surround the Sisters of Battle, take back a vital objective and launch a second attack to slay their commander. The Adepta Sororitas, however, have other ideas.

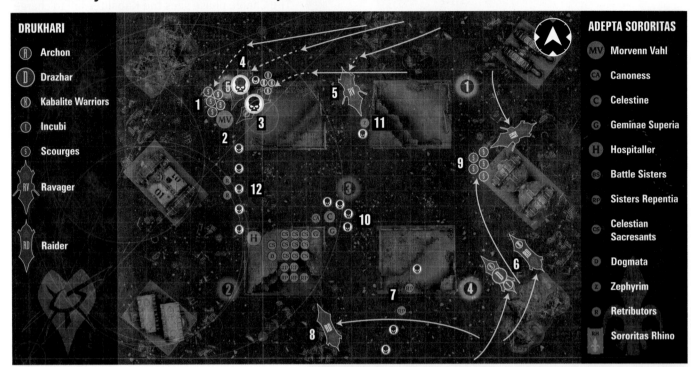

DRUKHARI

- (A) Archon
- (D) Drazhar
- (K) Kabalite Warriors
- (I) Incubi
- (S) Scourges
- (RV) Ravager
- (RD) Raider

ADEPTA SORORITAS

- (MV) Morvenn Vahl
- (CA) Canoness
- (C) Celestine
- (G) Geminae Superia
- (H) Hospitaller
- (BS) Battle Sisters
- (RP) Sisters Repentia
- (CS) Celestian Sacresants
- (D) Dogmata
- (Z) Zephyrim
- (R) Retributors
- (RH) Sororitas Rhino

TURN 1: LAWRENCE

With Morvenn Vahl now standing virtually on her own (and on an objective, no less), Lawrence made it his mission to take down the Supreme Commander of the Adepta Sororitas. 'If I can kill her this turn, I will score 4 VP for Assassinate,' says Lawrence. 'That's 3 VP, plus 1 VP for her being the Warlord. And I'll almost certainly retake objective 5 (see **Ours for the Taking**, right), giving me 12 VP for Take and Hold in the following round.'

In his Movement phase, Lawrence races the Scourges on the northern board edge (1) towards Morvenn Vahl (2). A Raider (3) and a Ravager (4) follow close behind, with a second Ravager in tow (5). Across the board, the Raiders that had moved south (including the one containing Drazhar) move back towards the eastern board edge (6) to avoid getting pinned down by the Repentia (7), though one Raider does fly over them (8) to put pressure on the units hiding in Stephen's main building. The last Ravager also moves back to target the centre of the battlefield.

Lawrence's Shooting phase is characteristically violent. The Scourges to the east (9) fire into the Zephyrim holding the centre of the board (10), killing all but the Zephyrim Superior who is slain by a dark lance from one of the Raiders. Nearby, the Kabalite Warriors and the Raiders they're mounted in account for three of the Repentia, but the last two Zephyrim (11) miraculously survive the barrage of shots aimed at them thanks to the use of a well-timed Miracle dice by Stephen.

OURS FOR THE TAKING

Objective 5 has been the most hotly contested objective on the battlefield since the start of the game. With the Sacresants dead, only Morvenn Vahl and a couple of Retributors stand between the Drukhari and their prize. Lawrence also has several Troops choices still alive in fast-moving vehicles, while all of Stephen's are dead by this point. It should be an easy prize to claim!

However, the most deadly of Lawrence's firepower is saved for Morvenn Vahl and the Sacresants (12), who Stephen positioned just close enough to act as her bodyguard (if they are within 3" of a character, that character cannot be the target of a ranged attack). Lawrence starts by blasting two of the Sacresants apart with one of his Ravagers' dark lances. He then targets them with the Scourges who fire a massive twenty-one out of a possible twenty-four shots with their shredders. 'If you could roll a load of ones now, please …' says Stephen, hopefully. 'Don't be like that, mate,' says Lawrence, laughing, 'We've had a good game so far!' Suffice to say, the Sacresants are obliterated by the Scourges.

With no one left to protect Morvenn Vahl, Lawrence turns the rest of his heavy weapons on her. His first Ravager causes just three wounds, but would probably have killed the Abbess Sanctorum had Stephen not used a Command Re-roll on one of his saves and a Miracle dice for another. Lawrence's last Ravager to fire causes two further wounds, taking her down to just one remaining. His last chance for a clean kill is the nearby Raider, which fails to wound Vahl.

'Combat it is then,' proclaims Lawrence. He charges Morvenn Vahl with the Scourges, a Raider and a Ravager (13), while the other Ravager to the north rams the Zephyrim hiding between the buildings. Lawrence chooses to fight with the Scourges first, reasoning that their higher number of attacks are more likely to kill Vahl than his

'If I can get to Morvenn Vahl and kill her, this turn could be absolutely mahoosive for me!' - Lawrence

vehicles' less numerous, but higher strength, attacks. They don't, as Stephen uses a Miracle dice to ignore the one hit that gets through. He then uses the Counter-Offensive Stratagem to interrupt Lawrence's fighting order. Morvenn Vahl smashes apart the Raider, which doesn't explode but disgorges four Kabalites and a broken corpse. The Ravager causes a single wound on Morvenn Vahl, but once again Stephen passes her save. He elects to fight with her a second time using her Righteous Repugnance ability; this time she obliterates the Ravager. 'You got really lucky killing all the Sacresants,' says Stephen, 'but the dice evened out, and I got lucky with Vahl's rolls. That one save might have cost you the game.' In other news, the other Ravager kills a Zephyrim.

LAWRENCE TURN 4 VICTORY POINTS

 48   **43** ⚜

Primary Objectives:
- 8 VP: Take and Hold
- 3 VP: Direct Assault

Secondary Objectives:
- 3 VP: Engage on All Fronts

Primary Objectives:
- DATA PENDING …

Secondary Objectives:
- DATA PENDING …

TOP TIP!
Lawrence: Always watch out for units that can fight twice (or potentially fight twice with the use of a Stratagem) in the Fight phase. Given the opportunity, a tactically astute player can move and charge their unit, pile in, fight, consolidate, pile in, fight again, then consolidate a second time. That's a potential gain of 12" just from pile-in and Consolidation moves – essentially a very long free move! A unit that wasn't on an objective at the start of your opponent's turn could suddenly be right on top of you. Beware of units that can shoot twice, too – that's always nasty!

BATTLE ROUND 4 CONTINUED: RIGHTEOUS RETRIBUTION

In which the Order of the Bloody Rose sally forth from their command building to bring the fight to their foes. Devout warriors are lost, but others are brought miraculously back to life.

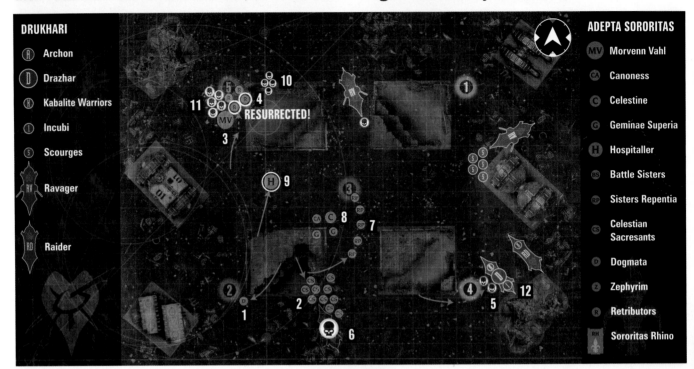

DRUKHARI

- Ⓐ Archon
- Ⓓ Drazhar
- Ⓚ Kabalite Warriors
- Ⓘ Incubi
- Ⓢ Scourges
- Ravager
- Raider

ADEPTA SORORITAS

- MV Morvenn Vahl
- CA Canoness
- C Celestine
- G Geminae Superia
- H Hospitaller
- BS Battle Sisters
- RP Sisters Repentia
- CS Celestian Sacresants
- D Dogmata
- Z Zephyrim
- R Retributors
- RH Sororitas Rhino

TURN 2: STEPHEN

With the enemy at the gates, Stephen finally commits the units that he'd held in reserve. In his Command phase, he uses the Dogmata's (1) Verse of Holy Piety to activate a sacred rite on the large unit of Sacresants (2). He picks The Passion, which converts every roll of a 6 in combat into two hits. To the north, Morvenn Vahl (3) gives the Retributors (4) re-rolls to hit and to wound.

Stephen's Movement phase could be described as explosive. The surviving two Repentia to the south (5) race forward and take objective 4 in the south-east corner of the board. Meanwhile, every Battle Sister currently inside the building in Stephen's deployment zone makes a swift exit. The Dogmata heads south-west to watch over objective 2, just in case Lawrence tries to claim it with the nearby Raider (6). However, Stephen also moves his large unit of ten Sacresants out of the building with the intention of charging said Raider! Meanwhile, his second unit of Repentia (who, up until this point, had not been seen) move out of the building and onto objective 3 in the centre of the board (7). By placing them in a crescent around Saint Celestine (8), Stephen ensures that she is protected both from shooting and melee attacks, but she can still make a Heroic Intervention if required.

Stephen's last moves see the Retributors move north to protect Morvenn Vahl and the Hospitaller (9) leave the main building to follow them. 'That might be a reckless move,' says Stephen.

TOP TIP!

Stephen: Acts of Faith – more commonly referred to as Miracle dice – are an absolute boon for Adepta Sororitas players. If you use them wisely they can get you out of the toughest scrapes. You can only acquire one per phase no matter how many enemy units you destroy, but you could, for example, almost wipe out a unit in the shooting phase, then finish them off in combat to gain a Miracle dice. High value Miracle dice are preferable, but in this battle I used a couple of 1s to automatically pass Morale tests (why risk failing?) and quite a few 2s to automatically pass Morvenn Vahl's 2+ save.

'Lawrence will probably shoot her, out there in the open on her own, but I really need to heal the Retributors so they can protect Vahl.' He spends 2CP (thanks to Agents of Vect) to play Rites of Restoration on the Retributors, bringing two back to life. Because of their proximity to Morvenn Vahl, she is now protected from the worst of Lawrence' shooting.

In the Shooting phase, the resurrected Retributors wipe out the nearby Kabalite Warriors (10). The Sacrosants and Dogmata cause two wounds on the Raider to the south, the former with their bolt pistols, the latter with a grenade.

Determined to get rid of the Raider, Stephen charges the Sacresants into it and plays the Tear Them Down Stratagem (Order of the Bloody Rose specific). Combined with the Dogmata's prayer, the Sacresants now receive additional hits on a hit roll of 6 and automatically wound on a hit roll of 6, too. They destroy the Drukhari vehicle easily. To the north, the Retributors join Morvenn Vahl in her fight against the Scourges (11). They kill one of their foes, who then strike back and wound Vahl once again. Stephen once more elects to pass her save with a Miracle dice. Morvenn Vahl easily kills off the other four Scourges!

Lastly, Stephen charges the unit of two Repentia into Drazhar's Raider (12). They cause a couple of wounds but are slain by the vehicle in return. 'That was a silly mistake there,' says Stephen. 'I just got caught in the heat of the moment!'

> 'I'm not going to get Celestine involved in the fighting. She's in a tight position, so she can just chill there.' - Stephen

STEPHEN TURN 4 VICTORY POINTS

 48　　　**66**

Primary Objectives:
- DATA ALREADY ACQUIRED

Secondary Objectives:
- DATA ALREADY ACQUIRED

Primary Objectives:
- 8 VP: Take and Hold
- 3 VP: Direct Assault

Secondary Objectives:
- 3 VP: Stranglehold
- 3 VP: Investigate Signal
- 6 VP: Bring It Down

BATTLE ROUND 5: CLIMACTIC CONCLUSIONS

Wherein the Drukhari unleash their deadliest killer, the Adepta Sororitas doggedly hold the line against overwhelming firepower, and a hero finally succumbs to their injuries ...

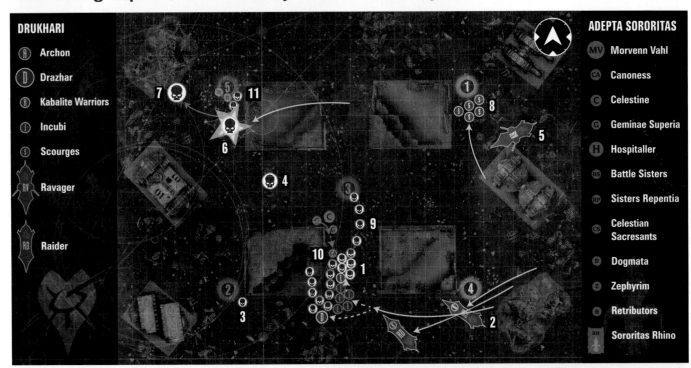

DRUKHARI

- (A) Archon
- (D) Drazhar
- (K) Kabalite Warriors
- (I) Incubi
- (S) Scourges
- (RV) Ravager
- (RD) Raider

ADEPTA SORORITAS

- (MV) Morvenn Vahl
- (CA) Canoness
- (C) Celestine
- (G) Geminae Superia
- (H) Hospitaller
- (BS) Battle Sisters
- (RP) Sisters Repentia
- (CS) Celestian Sacresants
- (D) Dogmata
- (Z) Zephyrim
- (R) Retributors
- (RH) Sororitas Rhino

TURN 1: LAWRENCE

Lawrence finally commits Drazhar and his Incubi (1)! He fires the dark lance on Drazhar's Raider (2) and kills the Dogmata (3), while the Hospitaller (4) is picked off by a Ravager (5). Lawrence even manoeuvres a Ravager (6) so that it can shoot Morvenn Vahl (7) as the closest target, but, once again, Stephen uses a Miracle dice to keep her alive. The Scourges (8) wipe out the Repentia (9). In the Fight phase, Drazhar and the Incubi make short work of the Sacresants, while the Ravager tries, but fails, to skewer Vahl on its pointy prow.

TURN 2: STEPHEN

Two major events happen in Stephen's turn. In the Fight phase, he charges his Canoness (10) into the Incubi, slaying four of them. However, he also retreats Morvenn Vahl from her fight with the Ravager and shoots it with the Retributors (11). They destroy it. It explodes, killing Vahl in the blast and earning Lawrence four victory points! On that explosive note, the game comes to an end with a narrow victory for the Adepta Sororitas!

BATTLE ROUND 5 VICTORY POINTS

72   83

Primary Objectives:
- 8 VP: Take and Hold
- 3 VP: Direct Assault

Secondary Objectives:
- 3 VP: Engage on All Fronts
- 10 VP: Assassination

Primary Objectives:
- 12 VP: Take and Hold

Secondary Objectives:
- 3 VP: Stranglehold
- 2 VP: Bring It Down

THE POST-BATTLE CHAT

After several hours of intense fighting, cunning tactics and good-natured banter, Lawrence and Stephen's battle comes to its grand (and extremely close) conclusion. They have much to talk about.

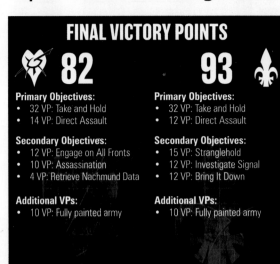

FINAL VICTORY POINTS

82   **93**

Primary Objectives:
- 32 VP: Take and Hold
- 14 VP: Direct Assault

Secondary Objectives:
- 12 VP: Engage on All Fronts
- 10 VP: Assassination
- 4 VP: Retrieve Nachmund Data

Additional VPs:
- 10 VP: Fully painted army

Primary Objectives:
- 32 VP: Take and Hold
- 12 VP: Direct Assault

Secondary Objectives:
- 15 VP: Stranglehold
- 12 VP: Investigate Signal
- 12 VP: Bring It Down

Additional VPs:
- 10 VP: Fully painted army

Lawrence: Wow! Now that was a very close game! There were so many swingy moments all the way through when either of us could have raced ahead to victory. It really came down to the wire, which is the best way to end a game, with both players invested in it right up to the end. I couldn't have asked for more!

Stephen: It was so close! Losing Morvenn Vahl and most of the Retributors right at the end of the game to an explosion almost cost me the battle, but I managed to hang on in there. It really felt like every single dice roll mattered – every kill, every advance move, every attack in combat was crucial by the time we got to the fifth battle round. What I'm really pleased with is that I stuck to my game plan. I discussed it with the Dwarfers while you were out of the room, and I doggedly pursued it right to the end. It's a nice feeling when you have a plan and it survives contact with the enemy.

Lawrence: Oh, it's like that is it? Getting tactical advice when I'm not around? I thought you were a pro! I think I also stuck to my game plan pretty closely, and it worked well, for the most part. I had a bit of a lead going into each turn, but what lost me the game was not killing Morvenn Vahl earlier. The turn when she should have died probably cost me the game as she scored Bring It Down for you and held on to that objective. Not only did you roll well for her, but you used your Miracle dice at exactly the right moment to keep her alive. I probably underestimated Vahl a bit in the early turns of the game, and I lost my Archon as a result. He could have killed her if I'd rolled well, but he didn't *and* she could have fought a second time if she needed to. I forgot that ability, and it cost me quite a few victory points later on.

Overall though, I'm really happy with how my army performed. Taking lots of units with the Objective Secured ability was hugely beneficial, and I really enjoyed having that flexibility on the battlefield. I knew that there was always another unit ready to swoop in and grab an objective.

Stephen: I totally agree, you played your army really well. I think you made fewer mistakes than I did throughout the battle, though. Moving the Hospitaller and the Dogmata out of cover at the end of the game cost me dearly as I gave up six victory points for Assassination. And what was I doing charging that Raider with my Repentia? They were desperate acts really – I'd had a few bad dice rolls in the preceding turn, and I didn't want to rely on my luck evening out. I erred on the side of caution, assumed the dice wouldn't cooperate and threw everything in for the final assault. I think it was prudent in the end.

Lawrence: Definitely. You played a really solid game and played the objectives well. You scored Take and Hold continuously throughout and scored maximum points for it in the last round. I think you picked your secondaries well, too.

Stephen: I really like the new secondary objectives. I can see Investigate Signal being a really popular choice for some armies, and the changes to Bring It Down were spot on for this mission against you.

Lawrence: I know! I didn't know about that change. In hindsight, I might not have taken so many Ravagers. Perhaps Trueborn with dark lances or units of ten Kabalites including them instead. There's always room to tweak an army list a little bit more!

THE ENEMY WITHIN

The galaxy is being torn asunder, new war zones exploding into life with ever-increasing frequency. As the worlds around the Nachmund Gauntlet descend into anarchy, the Imperium must remain vigilant for signs of that most hated foe: heresy!

Though all of the galaxy's warring races fight battles against myriad external enemies, some face another kind of threat. This they call the Enemy Within – traitors to the causes and peoples they once served. Indeed, many informed and influential beings the galaxy over would argue that the greatest danger to their society is not alien invasion but something far more insidious: corruption.

The Imperium is a colossal organisation, controlling over a million worlds spread out across the length and breadth of the galaxy and home to countless trillions of citizens. An unimaginably vast bureaucracy is required to have even a semblance of management of such a space and to try to keep order. It is little surprise that much falls between the cracks. The kinds of corruption that have blighted Human societies since time immemorial – bribery, nepotism, forgery, profiteering, fraud, extortion, exploitation – these are all endemic. They are all but impossible to stamp out and, provided that they do not impact on a world's ability to pay its required tithes or result in significant military defeat, are largely ignored by the powers that be.

THE DARKEST INFLUENCE

There is, however, a form of corruption that the Imperium cannot afford to give even a moment to breathe. The overwhelming majority of Imperial citizens have no idea that it exists, and this is no accident. Those of the Imperial bodies responsible for containing and quashing it have kept it secret deliberately, for even being aware that this form of corruption exists is to make oneself vulnerable to it. Knowledge leads to questions, and questions lead to doubt. A doubting mind, among other places, is where Chaos can seed itself and take root. The warp, known also as the empyrean, immaterium, and many other titles, is an ever-changing dimension of pure energy that lurks beneath the skin of realspace. It is here that every thought and emotion of the galaxy's sentient races coalesces in great tides and currents. It is a hellish place. Within its great storms and tempests live creatures known to Humanity as daemons, other-worldly beings who seek to corrupt and take over the minds and souls of the denizens of realspace.

It has always been known to Human beings that they are fallible, prone to error and vulnerable to vice. But even in the 41st Millennium, most are oblivious to just how frail and vulnerable they are. Chaos is so insidious that even those best guarded against it can fall into its dark clutches. It can take even the most noble of desires and twist them into terrible evil. It can exploit a Human's most fundamental needs, leading a person into the depths of depravity even as they still, entirely honestly, profess total loyalty and commitment to the Imperial cause. Even faith in the Emperor, which is seen by many who know of Chaos as being the ultimate personal safeguard, can be bent out of true by the power of the warp. Once something or someone has been tainted by the power of the warp, it spreads. What begins as a spiritual corruption and simple mutterings against the Emperor and the Imperium can lead to mass outbreaks of grotesque physical mutations and a proliferation of psychic abilities that are all but impossible to control. Murderous rampages, hideous plagues and full-blown insurrection soon follow.

Human fallibility has been a vulnerability even to advanced, well-ordered societies. For the Imperium, it is a gaping flaw. Its citizens are trapped in one of the most nightmarish, oppressive and hopeless regimes imaginable. Most would improve their lot if they could, at the expense of others if necessary. Should the means come to break out of their miserable existence, many would likely use it to gain any amount of power. The reality is that almost all would be wholly ignorant of the true danger of the power they are reaching out so desperately for.

All this can be exacerbated by the only form of faith sanctioned by the Imperium – that of the worship of the God-Emperor. Though to many it provides focus, meaning and purpose, for less scrupulous planetary officials and priests it is a tool, one they use to oppress their people. When many citizens turn to prayer and time and time again hear no answer or receive no aid, doubt creeps in.

THE HORUS HERESY

No instance of Human corruption has ever eclipsed that of the Warmaster Horus in terms of the sheer number of souls who were a part of it or the unimaginable devastation it caused. Though few in the 41st Millennium even know that Horus existed, let alone that he was for a time the foremost of the Emperor's Primarchs, he nearly brought what was then the fledgling Imperium to its very knees. Even those who do know of the Horus Heresy, or the Great Heresy as it is sometimes called, have very little knowledge of specific events and certainly no idea as to how it was that the Emperor's greatest champion turned against him. What is clear, however, is that Horus' rebellion shows that none bar the Emperor can be truly trusted. Even the most powerful beings ever created have demonstrated that they have weaknesses that can be exploited by the power of Chaos. Eight other Primarchs turned against the Emperor alongside Horus, all bringing with them their Space Marine Legions, vast fleets, and armies of countless billions of Human soldiers. Entire Knight houses and Titan Legions followed Horus willingly into civil war with loyalist forces, and forge worlds of the Mechanicum also swore allegiance to the banners of the Warmaster. The civil war that followed raged for years. The galaxy burned. Though the Emperor eventually won the final battle, he was mortally wounded and placed upon the Golden Throne. He remains there ten millennia later. Arguably, the Imperium has never truly recovered, and to this day enemies from that time still live to plague the realm of the Emperor, most notably Abaddon the Despoiler, formerly one of Horus' chief lieutenants.

Resentment, bitterness, despair and desperation take hold. Chaos, though the exhausted and oppressed Imperial masses will almost certainly not recognise it as such, seems to offer some small way for the lost to take control of their own fates. Yet these promises are lies.

The soldiers of the Astra Militarum too face incredible hardship that puts enormous strain on their minds. Many are seen as little more than assets to be expended. They fight in horrific conditions against heinous, terrifying foes. Many lose hope. Some come to believe the Emperor has abandoned them. Corruption can set in within the ranks for all manner of other reasons – depleted units may get merged with formations already tainted, agents of the Dark Gods may spread heretical teachings or rations may be poisoned with malefic tinctures. Some regiments find themselves afflicted with outbreaks of mutation. It can even happen by pure accident to soldiers truly believing they are being faithful to the Emperor and Imperium. Those slaughtering enemies in droves may find themselves aligned with the Blood God, Khorne. Those exposed to disease and malady, praying for salvation, may receive a response from the Plague God Nurgle but believe it is from the Emperor. Commanders wrapped up in conceiving cunning strategies may become acolytes of Tzeentch, the Architect of Fate. Obsession with victory, obedience, regimental honour codes or virtually anything else can serve as unwitting worship of Slaanesh, the god of excess.

Such is the danger presented by Chaos that should its followers be left unchecked, they could ultimately carry out rituals that would result in the unleashing of empyreal energies across vast regions of space. They can summon vast hordes of daemons, foul spawn of the Dark Gods who inhabit the warp. Entire systems can be pulled into the immaterium should the influence of Chaos grow strong enough. Thus, the Imperium has a number of shadowy organisations whose entire purpose is to root out and crush Chaos cults wherever they can be found in whatever form they have taken. Foremost amongst these is the Inquisition.

For ten thousand years, Inquisitors have been at the forefront of the Imperium's war against heretics, traitors,

renegades and mutants. Their word is absolute, their power almost unquestionable to all. Indeed, to even raise an eyebrow at the orders of an Inquisitor is to invite summary execution should the Inquisitor wish it so – for all true hunters of Chaos know that questioning is often among the first signs of sedition and taint. Inquisitors are among the few souls within the Imperium who have an understanding of how dangerous empyric corruption can truly be. Thus, they will stop at nothing to crush any hint of treachery and heresy wherever they find it. To fail is to invite mass slaughter, loss of worlds and even threaten the extinction of Mankind itself. Inquisitors have the power to order the death of millions to save billions and billions to save trillions. If taking a life guilty of heresy requires the death of a hundred innocents, then so be it. This is a trivial cost next to that of failure. The hard reality that all Inquisitors recognise instinctively is that, in a universe in which the Dark Gods are very real, allowing such notions as tolerance, freedom of religion and freedom of expression would, without doubt, result in the destruction of not only the Human race but of all realspace. The irony is that, even though it seems that the harshest methods are needed to ensure Mankind's survival, such measures can very easily push otherwise loyal citizens away from the Imperium. Many people crave freedoms that the Imperium would deny them, and for a significant proportion, being loosed from restriction would see them walk them directly into the embrace of Chaos. Indeed, some Inquisitors theorise that a desire for liberty in an individual is in fact nothing more than the temptations of the empyrean directly at work.

> 'A heretic may see the truth and seek redemption. They may be forgiven their past and will be absolved in death. A traitor can never be forgiven. A traitor will never find peace in this world or the next. There is nothing as wretched or as hated in all the world as a traitor.'

THE ORDO HERETICUS

The Inquisition is divided into many sub-organisations known as the Holy Ordos. All seek to preserve the Emperor and Imperium from threats both within and without. Some are more specific in what their Inquisitors surveil, such as the Ordo Astartes, who monitor the Space Marines, and the Ordo Barbarus, who monitor Human worlds with pre-industrial civilisations. Others, such as the Ordo Hereticus, have a modus operandi much wider in scope.

Founded in the aftermath of the Age of Apostasy and Goge Vandire's Reign of Blood, the Ordo Hereticus seeks out and fights the mutant, the witch and the heretic, leaving no stone unturned. A missing tithe, an unusually studious planetary governor, the slightest hint of popular movement amongst the masses – all can be readily attributed to any number of causes. Yet one such cause could be the taint of Chaos, and thus all must be investigated. Indeed, even if the taint of Chaos is not the root of these kinds of events, the Inquisitors of the Ordo Hereticus know it can most certainly be the end result if left unchecked.

THE MIGHTY FALL

A dark secret held by some in the Imperium is that even the Emperor's Angels of Death – the Space Marines – can fall to Chaos, despite years of psycho-indoctrination and mental conditioning. Should knowledge of such Heretic Astartes become widespread, it could shatter morale on thousands of worlds.

Space Marines are incredibly powerful individuals who have given up their very Humanity for Mankind. Their life is one of great hardship in which they will face uncounted horrors should they survive long enough. Their immense physical strength and mental fortitude gives them innumerable advantages over baseline Humans, and many in their lifetimes will face temptations to misuse that superiority. Some might decide they can rule a world better than the governor in charge. Many will believe that they can handle the revelations of certain knowledge forbidden to them.

Should Space Marines somehow be pushed over the edge of their phenomenal endurance, become disillusioned with their lot in the Imperium or give in to the temptations that come with their awesome power, the result is catastrophic. Years of repression gives way to a desire in the Space Marine to indulge every expression of their superiority. As beings who know nothing but war, and were made for nothing else, they continue fighting. They become pirates and raiders of the most dangerous kind. With their advanced equipment and enhanced physiques, they are all but unstoppable. Once servants of the Imperium, they now relish the opportunity to become true masters. Some even become tyrants of empires spanning multiple star systems.

There are other ways for Space Marines to turn against the Imperium. They may be wounded by a daemonic weapon, cursed with a malignant empyric hex or find themselves unable to expunge the thought of warp creatures they have encountered from their minds. The rot from within can progress extremely slowly before taking over completely. Even fighting traitor Space Marines can turn loyalists against the Emperor. Being near renegades who have embraced the power of Chaos can cause corruption in itself. Seeing the power that the traitors' new allegiance grants them also serves as temptation for some Space Marines.

No one truly knows how many Space Marines have turned against the Emperor since the Horus Heresy. Sometimes a single battle-brother from a strike force may turn. Sometimes entire Chapters abandon their oaths. Much-feared warbands now known as the Crimson Slaughter, the Brazen Beasts, the Angels of Ecstasy, the Scourged, the Flawless Host, the Purge, Adharon's Reavers and many others can all trace their origins to once-loyal brotherhoods of Space Marines.

JOIN THE FIGHT

FIGHT FOR THE EMPEROR! FIGHT FOR THE IMPERIUM! FIGHT FOR HUMANITY!

Inquisitors are figures of awe and fear, and the grim and gothic agents of the Ordo Hereticus are no exception. They spend their days studying texts that reveal the signs of the heretic and the mutant, or in excruciation chambers squeezing information from their prisoners. The monitoring of purity is the Inquisitor's greatest concern, and when they arrive on a planet, none there know where their merciless gaze may fall. Even other Inquisitors are not safe. An Inquisitor's abilities to access any vaults of lore they desire and to requisition any military forces they wish can, of course, go to their heads, for they too are Human. It is not difficult for individuals as discerning as Inquisitors to see danger in the behaviour of their colleagues, especially those who spend what they consider to be too much time with heretical texts. Entire wars have been fought between rival Inquisitors or Inquisitorial cabals over proper doctrine, and even though Inquisitors are possessed of formidable faith, strength of will and character, it is far from unheard of for one to turn against the Imperium. Such are the dangers of Chaos – it can even turn fortitude into a weakness to be exploited. A desire to do whatever it takes to preserve the Imperium can be twisted in the same way. Slowly but surely, more than a few Inquisitors have compromised on their principles to stamp out Chaotic cults only to sink into pits of depravity they cannot escape from without even noticing, ultimately becoming that which they once hated most.

TECH-HERESY

The Tech-Priests of the Adeptus Mechanicus are, and always have been, superstitious and ambitious in equal measure. In the deep past, many technologies developed by Mankind have proven to be too dangerous for their use to be permitted. Countless bizarre alien devices and artefacts tainted by the warp have been discovered by the Adeptus Mechanicus as well, the use of which is strictly prohibited. These restrictions have chafed at many Tech-Priests, who believe they can control whatever deadly powers might be locked away. In ancient, hidden files and datascrolls, there are records that claim that, as a part of his rebellion against the Emperor, Horus bought the loyalty of many Tech-Priests of Mars. He gave them priceless Standard Template Constructs from conquered worlds and played on techno-theological differences between various groups of Adepts to help provoke a schism. Most significantly, he promised that no field of technology would be closed off to the research of those who sided with him, even providing them with the means to open forbidden vaults sealed away for centuries untold.

Those who joined with Horus became known as the Dark Mechanicum, though many of its number refer to themselves as the New Mechanicum. Over the millennia, more rogue Tech-Priests and forge worlds have abandoned their allegiance to Mars, effectively becoming Dark Mechanicum as well. Without having to follow restrictions and laws laid down when the Emperor first allied with the Mechanicum, they have embraced any and every form of tech-heresy, even devising kinds that were never outlawed originally because none

thought them possible. Their experiments have grown more sick and twisted with each passing century, and the Dark Tech-Priests have become known for blending flesh, machine and daemon into horrific engines of war, such as arachnid Venomcrawlers, fire-breathing Heldrakes and hulking Maulerfiends. They have even fused daemonic entities with immense Titans, creating what must surely be among the most dangerous fighting machines in the galaxy.

THREATS MYRIAD

Those who have given up their faith in the Emperor and have turned to Chaos can be afflicted with unnatural deviance such as horrific mutations or come to venerate daemons themselves as deities. They may become agents of some or all of the Dark Gods. While falling to Chaos is the ultimate threat of corruption, it is not the only one. Xenos races too have the power to corrupt Humans in mind, body or soul. The ancient android Necrons can infest victims with swarms of minute mindshackle scarabs to entrap Human agents, or present themselves as gods to Human populations. Water caste envoys of the T'au Empire seduce Human settlements and worlds, turning the people against the Emperor to such an extent that many voluntarily become a part of the T'au Empire and join its military as so-called gue'vesa auxiliaries. Genestealer Cults are the most insidious. Using a method known as the Genestealer's Kiss, a single xenos vanguard organism can infect a huge number of people, causing them to venerate it as a divine Patriarch. Over time, generations of the infected breed all manner of Human-Genestealer hybrids who are fanatical worshippers of the Patriarch and do whatever it takes to serve it. Unbeknownst to the Genestealer Patriarch's deformed faithful, they are mere tools of still-more-nightmarish alien swarms that will soon descend to feed upon faithful and unbeliever alike. Other races include the Khrave, a single root mind of which has so much psychic power they can enslave an entire world. Against the threat of alien corruption, it is the Ordo Xenos of the Inquisition who takes the lead in the fight. Some know a great deal about many different alien races, turning their attention to whichever threats they deem worthy of their attention regardless of which xenos species presents the danger. Others become specialists, learning everything they can of one kind and seeking its defeat and eventual extermination over anything else. As with any other branch of the Inquisition, some Ordo Xenos Inquisitors see value in using alien technology and lore for their own ends, while others see this as just another form of corruption that must be uprooted and destroyed.

'We are at war with forces too terrible to comprehend. We cannot afford mercy for any of its victims too weak to take the correct course. Mercy destroys us. It weakens us and saps our resolve. Put aside all such thoughts. They are not worthy of Inquisitors in the service of our Emperor. Praise his name, for in our resolve we only reflect his purpose of will.'

– Inquisitor Enoch, *Castigations on the Last Days*

THE MARTYR'S REWARD

On the world of Aq'arus, Imperial forces are falling back in the face of a determined foe. The Khymer 64th, led by Major Jesmund Hesper, are all that stand between the retreat and total disaster, but will the Emperor protect them in their moment of sacrifice?

Major Jesmund Hesper stood atop an armoured bastion, wreathed in the light of the blessed candles that festooned its battlements. He gripped the edge of the crenellated parapet and wished fervently that he was down amongst the fighting. His Khymer 64th Infantry were spread out along a north-south line to either side of his position. Some were ensconced in armoured towers similar to his own. More crouched in the scant protection of earthworks that had been hastily blasted out of the ferrocrete approach to the Plenitus Spaceport.

Those soldiers were firing volley after volley out into the smouldering ruins of the Pilgrims' City, doing all they could to fend off the advance of the Shrouded. Heretic firepower came back at them, hails of autogun rounds mingled with shoulder-launched rockets and scatterings of mortar shells.

Meanwhile, at their backs, other loyalist regiments abandoned them one after another.

Hesper glanced over his shoulder as he heard the howl of lander engines rise to a crescendo. There went another of the lumbering troop transports, hauling itself off its landing pad in defiance of gravity and swinging its prow skyward. Thrusters flared incandescent in the Aq'arusian gloom as the huge vessel powered away into the heavens. Hesper watched it long enough to assure himself it had escaped the questing talons of flak that chased it, then felt a twinge of satisfaction. Each mass of soldiers successfully evacuated at least offered a measure of cold comfort that his own soldiers' deaths were not wholly in vain.

'Rearguard,' he made the word a curse as he looked back out at the fallen city. Those buildings not ablaze were obscured by choking smoke or lost in shadow, the sacred lumen of Saint Wynn having been thrown down and trampled by exultant cultists. How many Shrouded were out there Hesper didn't know, but he had no doubt there were far more than his depleted regiment could defeat. Even with the aid of the Sisters of the Radiant Pyre and what remained of the Heidrun 88th Armoured, this flimsy defence would not hold long.

'Orders are orders, Major,' said Commissar Qalo, standing at Hesper's back amongst his command squad.

'To flee, to abandon everything we have spent decades fighting for.' The Major didn't bother to keep the bitterness from his voice.

'No amount of firepower or bladework can halt a warp storm,' replied Qalo. 'Would you prefer we stay to be engulfed?'

'I wouldn't discount that fate yet, Commissar,' Hesper shot back. 'Without support, we may not be able to disengage when our own time comes.' He left the *if* unvoiced.

'The 64th will not fail,' said Qalo, and the absolute confidence in his voice shamed Hesper.

Thrusters bellowed again. Candle flames danced in the downdraft as another lander hauled itself skyward. Major Hesper barely had time to glance back at the craft, even now accelerating away from them towards the fringes of Plenitus Spaceport, before streaks of fire rose from the ruins to hammer its flank. The lander shuddered, listed to port, then plunged from its apogee.

'Oh, God-Emperor … Brace!' barked Hesper, ducking as the huge lander plummeted from the sky. Had it cleared the spaceport? Would it slam into the ragged columns of Imperial Guardsmen even now dashing for their own transports? Would it fall near enough that the fires of its demise would engulf the 64th?

Even through tightly closed eyes, Hesper saw the flash of the explosion. He felt the shock wave of the crash before he heard its avalanche roar. The bastion shuddered beneath him like a skittish beast, then was still.

The major rose slowly, staring over the frantic activity of the landing fields to the fresh inferno now raging amidst the ruins to the north. He shook his head, wondering how many loyal soldiers had met their ends trapped and screaming aboard the stricken lander. How many more cowering Imperial servants had been caught beneath it, people who had fled for the spaceport in the hopes of salvation, never realising that the Munitorum didn't consider them worthy of extraction? Perhaps it was better to endure swift and fiery annihilation than to be left amidst the ruins as the shadows closed in, or even to escape Aq'arus only to be swallowed up in a warp storm before they could reach the fabled Nachmund Gauntlet?

'Major, First Lieutenant Gwyll on the command channel reporting enemy push in her section.'

Voxman DuVayne's voice brought Hesper back from his reverie. He cursed and grabbed for his magnoculars, focusing on the far right of the line. There, Gwyll had dug her platoon in around one of the spaceport's access-arches.

He winced at the intensity of the firefight he saw. The hulking shapes of traitor tanks bulldozed through the ruins towards 1st Platoon's inadequate defences.

'DuVayne, tell the first lieutenant to hold fast. Lieutenant Jarus has the next section – have him detach his meltaguns to support her. And get me a line to Canoness Pheneloka. We'll need her to counter-attack swiftly if we're to throw them back.'

Hesper paced the tower-top, glancing up and down the line of the Khymer 64th as he waited for DuVayne to establish a connection with the Sisters of the Radiant Pyre. Another lander rumbled skyward, and then another. Wild chanting mingled with the madman's percussion of gunfire, carried on hot winds from the ruined city. His gaze strayed back to Gwyll's section, to the distant flicker of burning enemy armour and the flash-bloom of explosions tearing at Khymeran trenches. His impatience grew.

'I'm sorry, sir, no response from the Battle Sisters,' said Voxman DuVayne.

Hesper gripped the hilt of his sword, *Consequence*, tightly.

'Without their aid, First Lieutenant Gwyll will be overrun,' he said. 'Try again, DuVayne.'

'Yes, sir,' replied the Voxman, bending to her task.

'I'll take the reserve and get down there myself,' said Qalo. 'Eighth Platoon is still fresh.'

'If anyone goes, it should be me,' Hesper replied. 'Those are my soldiers, my responsibility. I have no right to stand up here in safety while they fight and die.'

'Your duty, Major, is to maintain the distance and strategic oversight required for proper command,' said Qalo. 'As you well know. You will not discard that responsibility in favour of wetting your blade in heretic blood, no matter how noble your reasons.'

'That's not …' Hesper began, then realised he had drawn *Consequence* several inches out of its scabbard in his desire to do violence. Taking a deep breath, he shoved the blade back into place.

He was about to speak when heavy calibre rounds stitched the battlements from somewhere amidst the ruins. Hesper ducked and cursed as stone shrapnel flew. Colour Sergeant Yorn crumpled, blood jetting from a gash in his throat. Medicae Usiah hastened to his side.

Over the hammer of gunfire and the chanting of cultists, Hesper heard DuVayne exchanging angry words with someone on the other end of her vox.

'Yes, I know that … No, I don't care … Yes, my commanding officer needs to speak to her now!'

Hesper beckoned for DuVayne to pass him the vox-horn, but she shook her head with a grimace.

'I'm sorry, sir. That was Palatine Mariahl. They've been ordered to take ship. They won't be coming. The Palatine recommended we embrace the martyr's reward that we have been offered.'

DuVayne's tone made clear that she shared Hesper's anger at these words. Of course the Adepta Sororitas would be pulled back first, he thought bitterly. They were more valuable than an under-strength regiment of infantry sloggers. Plenty more where the 64th came from.

'Orders,' said Qalo again, this time in a warning tone that brooked no dissension. Hesper noted that the Commissar's hands hovered near the holsters of his bolt pistols. Qalo's ice-white pupils glinted like chips of diamond in the candlelight.

The worst of it was that Hesper knew Qalo was right, just as he knew that the Battle Sisters were simply obeying the orders they had been issued from on high. There was no cowardice, only duty and obedience to a war machine that operated upon a scale so colossal as to sacrifice all compassion and humanity upon the altar of pragmatism.

'Don't worry, Qalo, we won't disgrace ourselves through dereliction of duty,' Hesper replied. 'Our faith is stronger than that.'

None of which lessened the dread of abandonment churning in the major's gut. He cast another look over the spaceport, noted the vanishingly small number of landers still idling on their pads. Sure enough, there were the surviving Adepta Sororitas hastening aboard their own evacuation transport. Hesper offered a prayer to the God-Emperor that one of those last few craft was allocated to his command.

'We are on our own, then,' said Qalo.

'Us and whatever's left of the Heidrun on the south approaches,' replied Hesper. The smile he received in answer was mirthless and knowing. If any Heidrun survived at this point, they might as well be on another world for all the help they would be. Hesper found his hand on the hilt of his blade again, the fingers of the other clenched into a fist. He couldn't slow the angry thundering of his heart, couldn't wholly restrain the need to hurl himself into the foe and cut them apart in righteous fury.

The look in Qalo's eyes told Hesper the Commissar knew precisely what he was thinking, and it was all the censure he needed to maintain his self control.

Barely.

'Commissar, take the Eighth, do what you can to aid Gwyll. *Damn* the time we wasted waiting for

reinforcements. DuVayne, get hold of command and secure our extraction order, quick as you can. Everyone who was getting out is gone, and I'll be damned if we get abandoned because the strategos forget us in their haste to save themselves.'

Commissar Qalo offered him an aquila salute and made for the stairway down to ground level, his augmetic leg clanking with every step.

'Make sure of the kill, Commissar,' Hesper called after him. Qalo raised a fist in response, and then he was gone. Hesper remained on the battlemented rooftop, prowling like a caged beast while DuVayne wrestled with her vox set and Medicae Usiah muttered the Emperor's grace over the dying Colour Sergeant Yorn.

'God-Emperor, we have always been faithful servants,' muttered Hesper, looking skyward in search of a star amongst the clouds and smoke. 'We have done your work, can do it still. Do not leave us here to the mercy of these heretics, I beg you. Don't make martyrs of us yet.'

The Khymer 64th endured another sixteen agonising minutes of combat before, at last, DuVayne was able to make contact with a harassed-sounding adjutant who confirmed the order to fall back. Major Hesper felt every second of the awful wait as fierce fighting raged along the trench line. One after another, his surviving soldiers were wounded or slain.

Now, as he led the retreat across the burning craterscape of the spaceport, he promised himself that if he ever got hold of the idiots who had left the 64th so long on the line, he would relieve them of their heads and damn the consequences. He wove around blazing wrecks and pushed through clouds of oily smoke towards the dimly glimpsed shape of the last lander in Plenitus Spaceport. With every moment that passed, he dreaded the sight of the ship rising on burning thrusters, abandoning them to their fate. His sense of desperate urgency caught like a stone in his throat, threatening to choke him and to plunge him into a state of panic in which he would be useless to his soldiers.

Hesper wouldn't allow that, not now. Not after the heroics of Commissar Qalo, limping along behind him with one arm thrown over a trooper's shoulders for support. Not after the way First Lieutenant Gwyll had held out against all the odds, paying for her tenacity with a head wound that saw her now borne insensible on a stretcher. Hesper hadn't time for a headcount, but his experienced eye told him the regiment had more wounded left than able-bodied soldiers, and with the Shrouded in close pursuit, this limping retreat would soon be overrun. But he wouldn't abandon his casualties. Major Hesper would be damned in the eyes of the God-Emperor before he failed his soldiers in such a fashion.

Ahead, a skein of smoke tattered apart, and Hesper felt a surge of hope as the lander was revealed. The craft loomed above them like a plasteel cliff. Its belly ramp was open, crimson light spilling out to limn the nervous-looking armsmen pacing at its foot. Hesper saw them spot the incoming Khymerans and begin beckoning frantically.

'And there I was … planning … to take it at a stroll,' grunted Qalo, his dry chuckle turning into a painful cough.

Hesper halted, turned, gestured to his retreating soldiers.

'Doubletime! Get yourselves aboard that lander, priority to the wounded. We—'

Bullets raked the Imperial Guardsmen from behind. A half dozen Khymerans fell, expressions of cheated dismay frozen on faces that had worn desperate hope moments before.

'Throne no you don't, not now,' snarled Hesper, tearing *Consequence* from its scabbard. He let his zeal and fury take over at last.

'Commissar, get the wounded aboard the lander,' he shouted, ignoring the bullets that whipped through the smoke. 'Fourth Platoon, Eighth Platoon, rearguard on me. Fighting retreat to the ramp. Let the heretics come! In the God-Emperor's name, the bastards will find nothing here but blood and death. Make sure of the kill!'

'Make sure of the kill!' echoed his soldiers as they fell into firing crouches around him and blitzed lasfire back into the smoke. Veiled figures swam into view, screaming and chanting as they bore down upon Major Hesper and his small but defiant rearguard. He shot a cultist through the face and then brought his blade up to impale another as the heretic charged him with a yell.

Hesper and his soldiers backed steadily towards salvation even as fire and smoke boiled around them, and the enemy's numbers doubled, then doubled again. The major was dimly aware of his wounded streaming aboard their evacuation craft, of the gap narrowing between him and safety, yet, in that moment, all he truly cared about was slaughtering these heretics who had cost him so much. He felt the righteousness of the killing flow through him. It lent fresh strength to his tired limbs, and he knew again that sense that the God-Emperor looked down upon him, just as he had that night in the shrine garden all those weeks before.

This time there was no sense of failure, nor of judgement. There was only the purity of the fight, and the knowledge that he was doing the God-Emperor's work.

'Blood and death!' he roared again, lopping the head from another Shrouded heretic. Somewhere on high, Jesmund Hesper was certain he felt the Emperor's approval swell like the warmth of a sacred candle flame against his skin.

THE FAITHFUL HOSTS

As the war around the Nachmund Gauntlet becomes ever more violent and destructive, miraculous feats are coming to light on both sides. Some can be attributed to the influence of the Dark Gods, while others must surely be a blessing from the God-Emperor.

he war in the Nachmund Gauntlet is becoming ever more desperate, with forces from both sides throwing everything they have at this vital warp route between the Imperium Sanctus and the Imperium Nihilus. As the war degenerates into a maelstrom of madness, miscommunication and slaughter, warriors on both sides must dig deep into their faith. Many call upon their chosen deities for the strength to defeat their foes, while others ask for protection from harm. Miracles are occurring with increasing regularity in the Nachmund Gauntlet, with martyrs on both sides rising from the ground to fight once more as blessed weapons, both fair and foul, are brought to bear.

THE RIGHTEOUS CRUSADERS

Over the next few pages, you will find new rules for using your armies in the Nachmund Flashpoint. These rules follow on from those published last issue, though they can be used independently if desired. Over the page, you will find eight new Stratagems that can be used by any army, including such miracles as They Are Risen!, which enables heroes to rise, seemingly from the dead, to fight once more. There are also four new Requisitions available to Crusading forces, plus a new psychic discipline for the most righteous psykers (whether good or evil). We particularly like Vortex of Holy Wrath, which is like a really, really angry Smite!

ABSOLUTION OF FAITH

In the previous issue of *White Dwarf,* we presented rules that allowed players to begin to take their Crusade force on a righteous journey of destruction through the stars. In this issue, you will find further additional rules that you can use in combination with those ones or in isolation (although we recommend using both together for the most complete experience). In this portion of their expedition, many of the elements of your Crusade force will have witnessed acts of incredible wonder, and increasing numbers are coming to see these as portents of things to come and validation for the rightness of your cause.

The rules you will find in this section are used for a Crusade force that is beginning to believe in its own holy mandate and starting to seek out divine aid on the battlefield. Some within your force will also try to spread this belief to those who have yet to experience the powerful boons and marvels that can be brought to bear in the name of your army's ideals.

RIGHTEOUS INSPIRATION

Whenever warriors are exposed to these significant events on the battlefield, their belief in their cause hardens. On the following pages you will find new Stratagems that represent incredible feats of martial prowess that capture the attention of the fighters who witness them, a collection of Requisitions that help to represent the impact this new knowledge is having on your Crusade force as a whole, and a new psychic discipline that contains a host of potent powers for the truly righteous to master.

All of these rules use Righteous Inspiration tallies on units' Crusade cards. Whenever you are instructed to add to a unit's Righteous Inspiration tally, if it does not have one already, create one for it on its Crusade card. Each time a unit has a Righteous Inspiration tally started for it, it also gains the **RIGHTEOUS** keyword.

During this stage of your Crusade force's journey, no unit's Righteous Inspiration tally can go above 8. If a unit's tally would go above this, any tally points in excess of 8 are lost.

STRATAGEMS

If your Crusade force has begun its Righteous journey, you have access to these Stratagems, and can spend CPs to use them.

STRENGTH OF PROVEN FAITH   [2CP]

Righteous Battle Tactic Stratagem

When a squad of warriors overcomes their enemies, they are filled with righteous pride. They have won and thus honoured their divine patron, who they know has granted them the strength to triumph and the resilience to survive. With this holy being by their side and watching their backs, they charge again and again into the fray, possessed of the strength of zealots fuelled by a noble cause.

Use this Stratagem in the Fight phase, when an enemy unit is destroyed by a unit from your army that has a Righteous Inspiration tally of 7 or less. Until the end of the battle, add 1 to the Attacks and Strength characteristics of models in that unit from your army. Add 1 to that unit from your army's Righteous Inspiration tally. Each unit from your army can only be affected by this Stratagem once.

SIGN OF THE DIVINE   [1CP]

Righteous Battle Tactic Stratagem

A holy mark appears before these warriors, bright and clear like a stream of pure spring water, showing them where the foe lies. Surely their divine patron has marked them out for great things.

Use this Stratagem in your Shooting phase, when a unit from your army that has a Righteous Inspiration tally of 7 or less is selected to shoot. Until the end of the phase, each time a model in that unit makes an attack, the target does not receive the benefits of cover against that attack. Add 1 to that unit's Righteous Inspiration tally.

A HOLY PRESENCE   [1CP]

Righteous Battle Tactic Stratagem

Despite almost overwhelming enemy pressure, a powerful presence holds these warriors firm, invigorating their weary bodies. Sure of the nobility of their cause, fear ebbs away as they take the fight to the foe.

Use this Stratagem in the Fight phase, when a unit from your army that has a Righteous Inspiration tally of 7 or less is selected to fight. If that unit is within range of any objective markers, until the end of the phase, each time a model in that unit makes an attack, you can re-roll the hit roll. Add 1 to that unit's Righteous Inspiration tally.

RIGHTEOUS RAGE   [3CP]

Righteous Battle Tactic Stratagem

Filled with zeal and holy wrath, these warriors desire nothing more than to purge the unrighteous who curse this world with their filthy presence. This is no time for mercy, no time for forgiveness – nought but the utter annihilation of the foe will satisfy their desire.

Use this Stratagem in your Shooting phase or the Fight phase, when an **INFANTRY** unit from your army that has a Righteous Inspiration tally of 7 or less is selected to shoot or fight. Until the end of the phase, each time a model in that unit makes an attack, add 1 to that attack's hit roll and add 1 to that attack's wound roll. Add 4 to that unit's Righteous Inspiration tally. You can only use this Stratagem once.

THEY ARE RISEN!   [2CP]

Righteous Epic Deed Stratagem

A great champion of your army falls and all are dismayed. And yet, before their very eyes, the hero rises, taking up weapons once more. Surely by this act, the divine patron smiles upon the entire host. What greater sign of their holy power could there be than the defeat of death itself?

Use this Stratagem in any phase, when a **CHARACTER** model from your army that has a Righteous Inspiration tally of 7 or less (excluding **VEHICLE** models) is destroyed. You can choose to roll one D6 at the end of the phase instead of using any rules that are triggered when that model is destroyed. If you do so, then on a 2+, set that model back up on the battlefield as close as possible to where they were destroyed and not within Engagement Range of any enemy models, with 3 wounds remaining. Add 3 to that model's Righteous Inspiration tally. You can only use this Stratagem once.

HOLY MISSION [1CP]

Righteous Epic Deed Stratagem

A psyker feels the power of their divine patron run through them – they have been chosen to perform righteous work. Holy warriors need healing; unclean foes need smiting. The task begins now.

Use this Stratagem in your Psychic phase, when a **PSYKER** unit from your army that has a Righteous Inspiration tally of 7 or less is selected to manifest psychic powers. Until the end of the phase, that unit can attempt to manifest one additional psychic power and you can re-roll Psychic tests taken for that unit. Add 1 to that unit's Righteous Inspiration tally.

DIVINE SHIELD [2CP]

Righteous Epic Deed Stratagem

No matter how brutal the melee, no matter how furious the foe, no strike they land seems to harm these warriors, who fight singing the praises of their divine patron. Clearly their unfailing faith has been noticed and rewarded.

Use this Stratagem in any phase, when an attack is allocated to a model from your army whose unit has a Righteous Inspiration tally of 7 or less. That attack has a Damage characteristic of 0. Add 2 to that model's Righteous Inspiration tally. You can only use this Stratagem once.

THE LAST RIGHTEOUS ACT [2CP]

Righteous Epic Deed Stratagem

Sometimes the devout warrior must fulfil their holy duties, even after their death has come. In these moments, their divine patrons preserve them for a little longer, knowing their devoted follower will carry out the necessary holy deed. All around witness the power of the divine beings when the battle-slain rise from the ground to perform one final sword thrust, axe swing or hammer blow.

Use this Stratagem in the Fight phase, when a unit from your army that has a Righteous Inspiration tally of 7 or less is selected as the target of an attack. Until the end of the phase, each time a model in that unit is destroyed, do not remove it from play – it can fight after the attacking model's unit has finished making attacks, and is then removed from play. Add 1 to that unit's Righteous Inspiration tally.

REQUISITIONS

If your Crusade force has begun its Righteous journey, you can spend Requisition points (RPs) on any of the following Requisitions in addition to those presented in the Warhammer 40,000 Core Book.

UNEXPECTED GIFT [1RP]

With much ceremony and praise, a largely unremarkable warrior is gifted a holy artefact by one of the host's most blessed fighters. Lost for words at such special treatment, the warrior is filled with pride and strives to prove themselves worthy of this divine honour in battle.

Purchase this Requisition at any time. Select one Righteous Relic (see *White Dwarf* issue 472) that a model from your Order of Battle has. Remove that Relic from that model's Crusade card and reduce its Crusade points total by 1. You can give that Relic to another model from your Order of Battle as long as that model does not have the **Righteous** keyword. Add 1 to the Crusade points total of the model you give that Relic to.

SHARING TIDINGS MOST GREAT [1RP]

Some squads of warriors witness countless miracles on the battlefield and often benefit from them. Such chosen fighters are filled with gratitude and hope, and they regularly share their experiences with their comrades as proof that their divine patron is with them, willing them to victory.

Purchase this Requisition at the end of a battle. Select one **Righteous** unit that was a part of your army for that battle to be the mentor and one unit without the **Righteous** keyword that was a part of your army in that battle to be the inductee. Roll one D6 for each point on the mentor's Righteous Inspiration tally, adding 1 if that unit has the **Character** keyword; for each 6+, add 1 to the inductee's Righteous Inspiration tally and it gains 1 experience point.

GLORIOUS CEREMONY [1RP]

Standing at the front of the host, a celebrated champion lifts their arms high and raises their voice in praise. The warriors gathered before them sing songs and recite prayers, each seeking to be heard by their divine patron. Some fall to the ground in subservience, tears pouring from their eyes. Even the most inhibited are slowly drawn into the power of the moment as the ceremony reaches a great crescendo of faith.

Purchase this Requisition at any time. Select one **Righteous Character** unit from your Order of Battle to be the ceremony leader, and one **Righteous** unit from your Order of Battle to be the ceremony participant. Roll one D6, adding 1 for each point on the ceremony leader's Righteous Inspiration tally; on a 1-6, the ceremony leader gains 1 Battle Scar; on a 7+, the ceremony participant gains one Righteous Battle Honour (see *White Dwarf* issue 472).

WONDROUS TEACHINGS [1RP]

Waking from a long and pleasant dream, the psyker realises the experience revealed knowledge and power previously unknown to them. The dream was surely a reward from their divine patron, granting them a portion of that being's holy strength.

Purchase this Requisition at any time. Select one **Psyker** unit from your Order of Battle that does not know a psychic power from the Righteous discipline (pg 97). That unit knows 1 psychic power from the Righteous discipline. Add 1 to that unit's Crusade points total.

RIGHTEOUS DISCIPLINE

Righteous Psyker units from your army can know psychic powers from the table below using the Wondrous Teachings Requisition (pg 96). You can either roll one D6 to generate the power, or you can select which power the **Psyker** knows.

When a **Righteous Psyker** unit from your army attempts to manifest one of the psychic powers below, if their Righteous Inspiration tally is 8 or more, add 1 to the Psychic test.

At the end of the battle:

- If a **Psyker** unit from your army successfully manifested any of the psychic powers from this discipline during the battle, add 1 to that unit's Righteous Inspiration tally.
- If a unit from your army was selected for one or more of the Blessing psychic powers from this discipline during the battle, add 1 to that unit's Righteous Inspiration tally.

1. LIVING BLESSING

The psyker summons into being angels of their divine patron. These wondrous creatures, invisible to all bar the psyker, aid their mortal allies, enhancing their blows and absorbing the strength of enemy attacks.

Blessing: *Living Blessing* has a warp charge value of 8. If manifested, select one friendly unit within 12" of this **Psyker**. Until the start of your next Psychic phase, add 1 to the Strength and Toughness characteristics of models in that unit.

2. AETHER WINDS

The psyker can see the great ley lines their divine patron has placed over this world to claim it as their own. The battlefield itself sits upon one, and its holy energies move at the behest of the psyker, allowing them to manifest tempests of righteous power.

Witchfire: *Aether Winds* has a warp charge value of 7. If manifested, select one objective marker within 18" of and visible to this **Psyker**. Roll one D6 for each enemy unit within range of that objective marker, subtracting 1 if that enemy unit has the **Character** keyword. On a 2-4, that enemy unit suffers D3 mortal wounds; on a 5+, that enemy unit suffers 3 mortal wounds.

3. SOUL LEECH

The souls of the faithless foes are ripe for plucking, to be offered up as gifts to the angels of the psyker's divine patron.

Malediction: *Soul Leech* has a warp charge value of 6. If manifested, select one enemy unit within 18" of and visible to this **Psyker**. Until the start of your next Psychic phase, each time a model in that unit makes an attack against a **Righteous** unit, that attack's hit roll cannot be re-rolled and that attack's wound roll cannot be re-rolled.

4. GUIDANCE OF THE DIVINE

The psyker's divine patron is a being of infinite wisdom and power, able to undo any of the psyker's foes. Knowing this, the psyker beseeches their master, humbly requesting knowledge of how to crush the hated enemy.

Blessing: *Guidance of the Divine* has a warp charge value of 6. If manifested, until the start of your next Psychic phase, this **Psyker** gains the following ability:

Guidance of the Divine (Aura): While a friendly **Righteous** unit is within 6" of this unit, each time that unit is selected to shoot or fight, when resolving that unit's attacks you can:

- Re-roll one hit roll.
- Re-roll one wound roll.
- Re-roll one damage roll.

5. VORTEX OF HOLY WRATH

The psyker summons into being a mighty vortex of power, the righteous anger of their holy patron made manifest. Terrible damage does it inflict upon the foe, yet true believers pass through it all but unscathed.

Witchfire: *Vortex of Holy Wrath* has a warp charge value of 7. If manifested, select one enemy unit within 18" of and visible to this **Psyker**. Roll one D6 for that unit and each other unit within 3" of it, subtracting 1 if the unit being rolled for has the **Character** or **Righteous** keywords. On a 2-4, that enemy unit suffers 1 mortal wound; on a 5+, that enemy unit suffers D3 mortal wounds.

6. GIFT OF HOLY FURY

The sight of the foe on the battlefield stirs much righteous hatred in the psyker. They know that such anger is a great power in its own right, and one that pleases their divine patron. Channelled into nearby allies, this holy fury spells doom for the foul enemy.

Blessing: *Gift of Holy Fury* has a warp charge value of 6. If manifested, select one friendly unit within 12" of this **Psyker**. Until the start of your next Psychic phase, that unit is eligible to charge in a turn in which it Advanced or Fell Back.

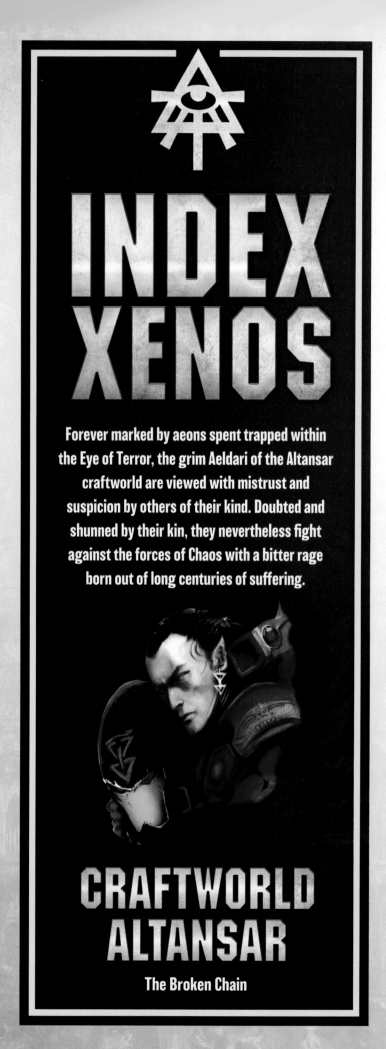

INDEX XENOS

Forever marked by aeons spent trapped within the Eye of Terror, the grim Aeldari of the Altansar craftworld are viewed with mistrust and suspicion by others of their kind. Doubted and shunned by their kin, they nevertheless fight against the forces of Chaos with a bitter rage born out of long centuries of suffering.

CRAFTWORLD ALTANSAR

The Broken Chain

Few of the Asuryani craftworlds have had a past as troubled and tragic as that of Altansar. Once trapped for millennia within the treacherous tides of the great warp storm that is the Eye of Terror, its people have endured horrors few other Aeldari can begin to imagine. Were it not for the legendary efforts of the Phoenix Lord Maugan Ra, the Harvester of Souls, the craftworld would remain confined within the Eye to this day.

After the Fall of the ancient Aeldari empire, the Altansar craftworld was close to the newly birthed Eye of Terror. Though they believed themselves safe enough, they were wrong. The Eye's borders – if such a term even makes sense for any warp phenomenon – are always in flux, ebbing and flowing unpredictably with all but unknowable empyric energies. It was in the pull of one of the Eye's tidal surges that Altansar was caught.

At first, the craftworld's Farseers, Bonesingers and voidmasters took every step they could to break their world-ship free from the hold of the immaterium, believing that, though they were in danger, they could escape. They were mistaken. Farseers and Warlocks were reduced to ash during psychic rituals designed to weaken the grip of the warp. Bonesingers worked themselves to exhaustion growing new, powerful engines and grafting them onto Altansar's flanks. Voidmasters spent countless hours pitting the world-ship against the empyric currents, analysing the flow of warp energies and the best firing patterns for their drives, hoping to grant their world-ship its freedom. Alas, every measure taken failed. The craftworld fell further into the Eye of Terror's clutches. Worse, in their expectation that the craftworld would break free, few Aeldari of the craftworld left when there might have been a chance to escape on smaller and faster vessels. For all this, Altansar's Aeldari continued to try every measure within their power to break their home free. The idea of being pulled into the Eye of Terror – the birthplace of She Who Thirsts and of their race's near-extinction – filled every citizen with the kind of dread and despair that would shatter the psyche of the strongest Human. For them, there was no option of giving up their efforts to escape or giving into the negative emotions they experienced.

As hope appeared to fade, things went from bad to worse. The runic wards surrounding Altansar's immense webway gates – each large enough for multiple spacecraft to advance through simultaneously – glowed hot. They burned so fiercely that many bent out of shape, either becoming all but unrecognisable or twisting into horrifying forms that drove weaker Aeldari to madness. Seeing this as a grim omen indeed, the Phoenix Lord Maugan Ra, born of Altansar and

'No Aeldari besides Maugan Ra are known to still live of those dwelling on Altansar at the time it fell into the grasp of the Eye of Terror. The Harvester of Souls has shared very little of what happened with others – even his fellow Phoenix Lords cannot be sure they know much of the truth of what happened to the craftworld. The Altansari themselves cannot claim to have full knowledge. So many who might have recorded their experiences were slain before they could put down their tales. Countless treasures from, and accounts of, that time have been destroyed in the innumerable battles the people of Altansar have had to fight to defend their home. What information that has survived to be in the possession of the Altansari in these dark days is so horrifying to them to read that few dare to try. Considerable tranches of it are metaphorical, allegorical or written in poetic form to protect future generations from the full horror of what happened in those days. Since their return to realspace, the people of Altansar have, like Maugan Ra, been far from forthcoming with the full tale of their loss to the warp. Thus my efforts to learn the truth have been stymied, at least in part, in a multitude of areas of study. What follows, regarding the tales of Altansar's fall into the warp and Maugan Ra's efforts to retrieve it, is the best I can collate – yet it remains a collection of rumours, murmurings and tales woven together through careful assessment, meditation and many castings of the runes.'

– Eldrad Ulthran

aboard the craftworld since its strife began, mobilised hundreds of Dark Reaper Aspect Warriors, his own followers, to guard the webway gates. The Harvester of Souls' actions troubled the people of Altansar greatly. Even then, relatively soon after the Fall, the Asuryani held the Phoenix Lords in the highest esteem. If such a warrior summoned so many others to their cause, it must surely have been a desperate one. The craftworld's troubles were just beginning.

THE RUNES BROKEN

For many years, Farseers and Warlocks of Altansar worked to repair the runic wards protecting their craftworld's webway portals. With each passing day, more work was required. Though carefully crafted and imbued with awesome psychic power only Aeldari with centuries of experience could control, each new rune was twisted more quickly than the one it was intended to replace. Eventually, each psychic ward was being unmade faster than a replacement could be fashioned. Inevitably, whatever force was causing the runes to be broken was too powerful for those that remained to contain and would soon reach critical mass. Despite the efforts of Altansar's most powerful seers to read the runes of fate and fortune, none knew what the future held for their craftworld. Even the least of their fate-readers, however, could see that terrible hardship was likely coming. A great sense of foreboding fell over the Altansari.

Through this period of agonised waiting, all looked to Maugan Ra. For not a single second had he let his vigilance falter as he stood watch over the webway gates. Many thousands of the

craftworld's people took up the Path of the Warrior in this time, more than half becoming Dark Reapers. In Maugan Ra, the most grim and morbid of the Phoenix Lords, they saw their only true hope. War was coming to the craftworld, and all of its citizens knew that this could be the war that decided whether Altansar lived or died.

At long last, the remaining runes that still held out on the webway gates flickered and grew dim, emitting acrid smoke as they dropped to the ground, charred deepest black. In that moment, all of the webway portals came alive. They did not shimmer with cerulean light as they once had. Instead, the energy contained by the gates glowed in every shade of purple, appearing to bubble and pop like thick, sucking mud close to a thermal spring. It was the moment Maugan Ra had been expecting.

THE BROKEN CHAIN

The world-rune used by Craftworld Altansar is known as the Broken Chain. This is not only a reference to the story in Aeldari myth of the escape of Kurnous and Isha from the dungeons of Khaine but also the shattering of the links that Khaine used to bind the smith-god Vaul to his anvil. This symbol represents to the Aeldari – among many other things – that they might not be doomed to the same fate as their ancestors, that they can control their urges and be free of them. To those of Altansar, this symbol also became a reflection of their eventual escape from the Eye of Terror. Since then, they have added the broken infinity loop to the world-rune, placing it above the Broken Chain.

MAUGAN RA

Of all the pupils of the first Phoenix Lord, Asurmen, it was Maugan Ra who fell furthest from the fold in his interpretation of his mentor's teachings. More than any of those who would become Phoenix Lords, he embraced the art of killing foes from afar before they could strike back, crafting baroque, sinister ranged weapons that defied categorisation. Maugan Ra learnt that even the mightiest and most outlandish of weapons could be used with the same precision as Kurnous unleashing his hunting arrows, provided the warrior wielding it was skilled enough. It was the knowledge that the kiss of death can be delivered from a distance with grace and ruthless efficiency that Maugan Ra taught his disciples, and this became the central credo of the Dark Reapers Aspect. His followers exemplify the war god Khaine in both his far-reaching fury and his aspect as destroyer. They aim to embody Khaine's spear, hurled across worlds to strike at those who consider themselves beyond the Aeldari's reach. For the Dark Reapers, precision and

attaining the perfect shot is everything. In the many battles for Altansar, they would rely upon these skills time and time again.

Maugan Ra is the only living Aeldari known to have escaped Altansar before the craftworld was drawn into the Eye of Terror. Though never to his face, some Aeldari whisper that his time so close to the warp storm left him touched by darkness. Maugan Ra cares not for these rumours, and, though he is a figure of fear amongst his people, he lets his actions show where his loyalties lie. He cut down the Daemon Prince Periclitor in the Ybaric Cluster. On the honeycomb world of Knesh he defeated the Red Wyrm. Standing alone, he triumphed over swarms of Tyranids from Hive Fleet Leviathan threatening a webway gate on Stormvald. During the Thirteenth Black Crusade, he fought beside the strike forces of Craftworld Ulthwé, slaughtering followers of the Dark Powers in droves. Maugan Ra has also stood beside the Ynnari, fighting against the forces of the Thousand Sons Traitor Legion in the webway, along with other Phoenix Lords.

Maugan Ra wields the Maugetar, 'the Harvester'. This unique weapon fires plate-sized, mind-linked shurikens covered in bio-toxins so virulent they cause their victims to detonate, even after the merest graze. Should any foes survive to dare assail him in person, the Maugetar is fitted with a deadly, scythe-shaped reaping blade – a weapon so sharp it can disembowel Ork warbosses and behead Tyranid synapse creatures in a single swing. There are many tales and legends as to how the Maugetar was crafted, and only the Harlequins tell them. These agree on only one point: that it was the Harvester of Souls himself who made it. Some say Maugan Ra abducted the legendary Bonesinger Kaeleth-Tul and forced him to teach him all he knew of weapon-smithing. Others say the Phoenix Lord fought his way through millions of daemons upon an old Aeldari world to claim a scythe-shaped piece of blended starmetal and wraithbone, which he tempered in the molten blood of an Avatar of Khaine. Every such tale is dark and sobering to the Aeldari, speaking of sacrifice and fratricide of such ruthlessness that it surely must have split Maugan Ra's soul in two.

A CRAFTWORLD AFLAME, A CRAFTWORLD AWASH WITH BLOOD

Not idly had Maugan Ra maintained his vigil nor silently. Each day, seers and Autarchs of the craftworld came to him, seeking his wisdom and appraising him of tactical plans, weapon manufacture and warrior musterings. The Harvester of Souls told them of his own strategies. The craftworld had to be defended from enemies without – those coming from the Eye – as well as those within. The Phoenix Lord knew that something was coming.

The first daemon to spill out from Altansar's tainted webway gates was blown apart in a shower of black warpstuff before it could fully emerge. Maugan Ra claimed that first kill – it would be very far from his last. Hordes of the neverborn followed, only to be blasted to ruin by the disciplined volleys of Dark Reapers who had taken up key firing positions. The Aspect Warriors delivered rockets in fields of overlapping fire like symphonies of death. When warriors of one shrine retired for reloading and rest, others returned to the fight, ensuring not a single second of reduced firepower against Altansar's daemonic invaders.

At the first daemon's appearance, alarm ran through the craftworld that warpspawn had breached it. Battle plans long in the making were brought into action: Aspect Warriors raced to arm themselves; Guardian militias were activated; armouries came alive with activity as weapons and armour were distributed and grav-tanks, jetbikes and War Walkers readied for war. With heavy hearts, Spiritseers plunged into the infinity circuit, plucking out the most warlike souls for implantation into wraith constructs newly produced in droves by the craftworld's Bonesingers. The thought of so many of Altansar's dead being taken from this spiritual haven sickened the craftworlders to the core, but they recognised they had little choice. The world-ship was at stake, and, if they were to survive, the Asuryani could not afford the luxury of discretion in this regard. Meanwhile, the Avatar of Khaine's chamber pulsed with a lust for war, and that year's Young King was taken to it in preparation for rousing the shard of the Bloody-Handed God.

The first horde of daemons to force their way into Altansar was defeated at the webway portals – Maugan Ra did not even have to utilise the blade affixed to the Maugetar. But many more came. The strength of each wave varied, depending on the warp's fluctuating hold over the craftworld, but all were larger than the first. Even with much of the world-ship mobilised for war – and the Bonesingers and smiths producing weapons, ammunition and vehicles at a prodigious rate – the Altansari were pushed back as the months and years went by. Sometimes the warp energy sustaining a horde of daemons would grow too weak after a handful of hours, and levels would not increase to sustain warpspawn for months. At other times, such would be the strength of the empyrean that the daemons would be able to appear and fight continuously for days or weeks, with barely a few hours of reprieve for the increasingly exhausted defenders before the next attack came. This went on for decade after decade, and, over time, the strength of the invading daemonic hordes grew. The number of Altansar's dead was so high that many funerary rites were abandoned. Corpses were burned in great pyres, and the spirit stones of hundreds were taken to vacant wraith constructs even before being placed within the infinity circuit.

As the time between each wave of daemons grew shorter, and as casualties mounted, it became all but impossible for Altansar's armies to recapture lost areas of the craftworld before the next horde struck. As the world-ship was pulled closer to the Eye of Terror, the power of the immaterium grew strong enough at times for daemons to manifest spontaneously in different areas of the craftworld, making it increasingly difficult to establish firm battle lines and mount a defence. Through it all, Maugan Ra was at the forefront, slaughtering daemons by the score with every volley, leading devastating counter-attacks and holding to the last to ensure the evacuation of citizens from threatened areas. Slowly but surely, however, the craftworld was falling to the enemy. The Gardens of Lileath at Rest were turned from a peaceful haven into a place of terror as lush floras of every kind were warped into sentient, flesh-hungry predators. The Shadowmoon Forest, despite a valiant defence on the part of hundreds of Striking Scorpions and Rangers, burned with lilac, crimson, violet and teal flames that never extinguished. The Shrine of Asuryan was desecrated with Aeldari blood as every last one of its defenders was torn to shreds by packs of ravening Flesh Hounds. The Tri-spire of Transcendence was taken over by daemons of Slaanesh, who turned a place of wisdom and meditation into a depraved torture chamber – no Aeldari of Altansar suffered more than those unfortunate enough to find themselves there. The Watchtowers of the Onyx Flame, Vermilion Falls and Cerulean Stone fell in turn to spreading masses of Plaguebearers. Their once-proud wraithbone was reduced to decaying rubble, and the flesh of the Aspect Warrior and Guardian garrisons mulched and warped into bloated fungi, the spores of which caused a hideous psychic malady that infected and slew thousands slowly and painfully.

The Altansari were losing. Maugan Ra knew it. Though he would never dare reveal it to the Aeldari around him – who looked to him more than any other to see them through their strife – he too was exhausted and felt the long, sharp claws of despair scrape the back of his mind. He dared not let it take hold. When, at long last, Maugan Ra was forced to withdraw his warriors from the Drakion Gate and the Fortress of the Ivory Sword to ensure that the Dome of the Azure Star did not fall into the hands of daemons of Tzeentch, he knew his forces would have to strike back soon or the craftworld would be lost. It was clear that there was little chance they could ever fully push the daemonic horde back and fully repair the warding runes on the webway gates. To his mind, nothing less than the permanent sealing of the portals would suffice.

THE BARRING OF THE GATES

Had any besides Maugan Ra made the proposition he made to the craftworld's remaining Autarchs and Farseers, they would have been met with the scornful laughter of those exposed to far too much hardship. Instead, as Maugan Ra spoke of his intention to shatter the link between the warp and the craftworld's webway gates, all listened in silence. Many had suffered wounds in the craftworld's defence, and all were visibly drained. The burden of living to potentially see their home obliterated beneath a tide of daemonic filth weighed so heavily upon their shoulders that their very postures had changed: few sat tall in their chairs with the haughty pride that comes naturally to the Aeldari. He knew they needed a real victory – one that would give them hope.

Maugan Ra declared he would take a mixed force of Aspect Warriors and seers to the webway gates during the next receding of empyric energies. There, they would seal or destroy the portals.

This was a desperate measure – one that would likely separate Altansar from the rest of their kind for millennia – but the daemons were innumerable. Striking Scorpions and Warp Spiders moved ahead of the main force, destroying pockets of lingering daemons and distracting others as the main Aeldari contingent advanced. Maugan Ra accompanied this latter group, consisting of Dark Reapers, Fire Dragons and seers.

The party moved swiftly, knowing that at any minute the tide of the warp could swell once more and unleash new waves of daemons upon Altansar. They passed corpse-choked halls and walls out of which Aeldari faces peered, contorted into expressions of silent agony. Tortured wraithbone pulsed with corruption everywhere, and questing tentacles writhed and wriggled in nested clumps, threatening to seize incautious warriors. But the worst sights were the shattered spirit stones and the Aeldari who still lived in these tainted regions. Many had been driven to insanity, overcome with bloodlust or possessed by dark spirits. They attacked Maugan Ra's warriors with wild abandon, scratching at armour with their bare hands, snarling, biting and frothing at the mouth. With terrible sadness, the Aspect Warriors put these Aeldari out of their misery.

The bulk of Maugan Ra's forces reached the webway gates intact. Here the power of the warp was at its strongest anywhere in the craftworld. The heads of the psychically sensitive Aeldari pounded due to the strength of the energy. Some of the seers and Warlocks, even more sensitive to the empyrean than their fellows, fell to their knees, clutching their heads in pain. Maugan Ra ordered Fire Dragons to plant fusion charges upon the

webway gates and other warriors to take up watch around them. Scarcely had the Fire Dragons commenced their work when daemons began pouring from the portals. Battle erupted as other Aspect Warriors sought to shield the Fire Dragons. Dark Reapers poured rockets into the oncoming warpspawn. Striking Scorpions dived between the daemons and the disciples of Fuegan, intercepting neverborn with their whirring chainswords. Warp Spiders flickered in and out of reality, leaping wherever enemy pressure was greatest to unleash clouds of monofilament wire before jumping to their next targets. With each passing second, another Aeldari life was snuffed from existence as more and more daemons poured through the gates. Maugan Ra had brought a strike force on this mission, not an army. They did not have the numbers for pitched battle. He himself was in the heart of the fray, sweeping the Maugetar in great arcs that cut through several warpspawn with every swing. Whenever there was a break in the combat, he unleashed hails of shurikens to cut down dozens more. Seconds felt like hours as the Harvester of Souls urged his warriors on. Fire Dragon Exarchs told him that the charges were now set, but some Aeldari would have to stay with them until their detonation. Already, darkly intelligent daemon lords had begun to direct packs of their minions towards the charges' locations.

Maugan Ra cursed at the thought of yet more Aeldari being slain. He remained fighting until the last possible minute before withdrawing. The fusion charges detonated in a blinding flash of searing light that scorched his armour. Scores of Aeldari were disintegrated and hundreds of daemons were banished in an instant. The collapse of the portals unleashed a temporary burst of power, as energy contained by the wraithbone constructs was unleashed. Maugan Ra had retreated enough that he was only knocked to the ground, but much of the chamber was completely obliterated. Yet somehow one webway gate remained intact enough that daemons were still intermittently breaking through. Without hesitation Maugan Ra levelled the Maugetar, taking careful aim at the greatest weakness in the structure, and unleashed a volley of hundreds of shurikens. The intense fire finally collapsed the wraithbone gateway, and the roiling energies it contained flickered out of existence. No longer could daemons storm Altansar through its webway portals.

RELUCTANT FLIGHT

With the webway gates destroyed, Maugan Ra and the handful of survivors returned to their kin as heroes. Though they were still occurring, daemonic attacks had been significantly reduced. When the Phoenix Lord attended the craftworld's council to discuss plans for the recapture and cleansing of the rest of the world-ship, the seers and commanders told him that whether his plans succeeded or failed, he would not be on the craftworld to see. In secret, the council had ordered the craftworld's most famous and skilled Bonesingers to craft a void ship capable of escaping the Eye of Terror's near-intractable grasp. It had taken them more than two centuries, enormous effort and many resources, but they had succeeded. The council told Maugan Ra that there was no hope of the craftworld ever escaping, and they would not allow a disciple of Asurmen to be lost as they would be. They implored the Harvester of Souls to tell the rest of their kind what had happened to them and said that they would never give up hope that one day he would find a way to recover them and return them to the galaxy.

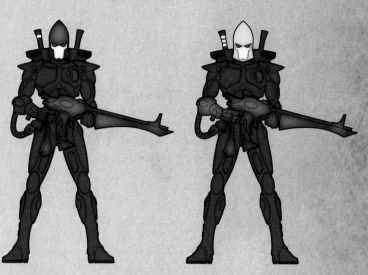

For hours Maugan Ra protested, exhibiting a frustration and anger rarely seen from the darkly composed and distant Phoenix Lord. The Aeldari around him refused to concede, though it clearly pained them greatly to deny the living legend before them – one who had done so much for his people. Eventually, it was the words of Autarch Elithinel Ullathani who persuaded him. Once, she had been a Dark Reaper under his tutelage, one of the finest he had ever taught. She had gone on to great things, succeeding in both the Fire Dragons and Swooping Hawks Aspects before taking up the Path of Command. Ullathani spoke with both eloquent grace and the undeniable firmness of one long-experienced in leadership. She told him that, while his craftworld would miss him dearly and long for reunion, he could do more for them by escaping and returning to pull them from the great abyss they headed towards so inexorably. Finally, she said that there was little he could do for the Altansari now, but that he could do much for the Asuryani of the rest of the galaxy. At long last – with some legends stating that he had tears forming in his eyes – Maugan Ra relented. He agreed to depart, vowing he would one day return and save the people of Altansar.

Within two centuries, Altansar was pulled fully into the Eye of Terror. Five hundred years had passed since the power of the warp first took a hold over the craftworld.

THE RETURN

Thousands of years passed. Despite never giving up his search and fighting for the Aeldari on countless battlefields, Maugan Ra could not find what he longed for more than anything else: the means to recover his lost craftworld. Yet he did not give in to the nagging feeling that, as time progressed, the people of Altansar might all be lost forever.

After millennia of warfare and waiting, Maugan Ra's chance finally came during Abaddon the Despoiler's Thirteenth Black Crusade. The forces of Chaos, spat out from the Eye of Terror as they were, left a gaping lesion in space where realspace and the warp could coexist. This created an opportunity not only for Maugan Ra to enter the Eye but also for Craftworld Altansar to escape it. With colossal battles raging around the Cadian Gate, forces on both sides were more than distracted; there was no better chance for the Harvester of Souls to plunge into the Eye. Thus he undertook the perilous quest to find his home. The tale is recorded in the macabre Bás-Finscéali lays. These speak of his followers, a band of courageous Asuryani named the Hanndroth Bhanlhari – the Avengers of the Lost Clan taking the Quest Eternal – including Dark Reapers, Swooping Hawks, Warlocks, and warriors from Ulthwé, Mymeara, Kinshara and other craftworlds.

In the great odyssey that followed, none of Maugan Ra's followers survived. The Bás-Finscéali, allegorical and metaphorical as they are, record that Maugan Ra left a silvered trail of soulfire in his wake through the Eye of Terror. They tell of his slaughter of the Thousand-eyed Beast, his toppling of a creature known only as the Plague Gholem and his successful answering of the eleven riddles of the Gyre-Sphynx of Pheba-Korinteias. Long, winding and arduous was the path the Harvester of Souls followed, and countless were the foes and obstacles that it is said he had to overcome.

At long last, Maugan Ra finally discovered Altansar, or what remained of it. For thousands of years, its people had navigated the Eye of Terror, avoiding raiders, daemons and would-be conquerors, fighting for survival in the most hellish environs any Aeldari could begin to conceive. Though not one of the Altansari Maugan

Ra once knew still remained amongst the living – and he could tell with a glance that these survivors were very different from the Aeldari he had once fought beside – he was overjoyed by his discovery. Following his silvered trail, he brought Altansar out of the Eye of Terror and into the relative safety of realspace for the first time in thousands of years.

Despite the near-miraculous recovery of a craftworld once thought lost to a dying people, there was no celebration or welcome for Altansar upon its return. Its citizens were treated with open suspicion by other Aeldari. Even though the Altansari constructed a new webway gate to connect themselves with their kin, most were forbidden from journeying to other craftworlds and were even met with hostility. Many outside Altansar raised the question – though never in Maugan Ra's presence – of how any Aeldari could be left untainted after what the Altansari had suffered and how they could have survived. Despite the proven loyalty of the those of Altansar over many battles since their craftworld's return, even now some Aeldari dare wonder if their professed alignment with craftworld culture is exaggerated, and if they are not in fact in allegiance with Slaanesh. Altansar is not helped by the fact that millennia within the Eye of Terror saw them turn to pragmatism over tradition whenever a conflict between the two arose. To stay alive, many ancient ways and rites were put aside for the sake of expediency. Though many of the returned craftworlders are slowly resuming the discarded rituals, large numbers of Asuryani view the Altansari as disdaining of tradition, and as a result they look upon them with a mix of scorn and deep distrust.

DAYS OF THE DATHEDIAN

Regardless of the truth of their purity, it is undeniable that spending millennia in the Eye of Terror altered the people of Altansar. Most refuse to remove their helmets in the presence of Aeldari from other craftworlds, and those few who have revealed themselves have features so deathly pale that they seem to be trapped in some kind of shadowy half life. This has led some Aeldari to surmise that the Altansari must have made some pact with Ynnead, God of the Dead. This theory has gained some traction, fuelled by rumours hailing from Ulthwé. The stories tell of an Altansari Warlock who, during the trial of Eldrad Ulthran, claimed that her world-ship only survived because of a shroud Ynnead placed over it and its people. The rumours go further to say that, shortly after this revelation, the Warlock dedicated her soul to Ynnead and Yvraine – the god's emissary – before taking her blade to her own throat. Whatever the truth of this story, what is known is that Altansar has thrown its weight behind the Ynnari cause, its warriors fighting with them on multiple occasions.

The Altansar craftworld itself is but a shadow of its former glory. To this day, more than two-thirds of its space remains quarantined, rune-wards shielding the rest of the world-ship from the empyric taint that remains. Warriors remain vigilant at all times for any signs of daemonic encroachment on those areas of the craftworld deemed safe. Even since their escape from the Eye of Terror, Altansar's warriors have had to contain daemonic outbreaks from the long-destroyed Fortress of the Blazing Suns, the Chamber of the Crimson Spear, and others. This they have done in secret, knowing that to tell other Aeldari of what has become of their home would only see them further shunned. Only select members of the Ynnari have been allowed to visit Altansar, including many Bonesingers, whose skills are vital if the craftworld is to rebuild in such turbulent times as these.

Altansar is a highly militarised craftworld, with almost all other roles seen as secondary to those relating to war. Its armies rely heavily on infantry as huge numbers of its vehicles were destroyed over the millennia, particularly in the early fighting against daemonic invaders, and the craftworld has had limited resources to replace them. A significant proportion of Altansar's Aspect Warriors are Dark Reapers, in honour of the Phoenix Lord who did so much to preserve the craftworld and who fulfilled his oath to rescue it. Many others are Swooping Hawks, in tribute to Baharroth, the Phoenix Lord with whom Maugan Ra shares the closest bond.

Such has been the unrelenting need for ghost warriors to defend the craftworld that Altansar's people have long since lost the revulsion for utilising wraith constructs that even the Aeldari of Iyanden retain. Indeed, wraith warriors have become a part of life for the Altansari, with all but a handful of individuals resigned to the fact that death will offer their souls no rest. The return to realspace has meant that a small minority on the craftworld's ruling council are pushing to return to the old ways, under which the utilisation of wraith constructs would be a rarity, rather than a given. But with Altansar waging a relentless war against the forces of She Who Thirsts, and even now committing its strength to the growing conflict surrounding Sangua Terra, their voices remain quashed by the vast majority of their peers.

Those of Altansar say little of their terrible experiences in the Eye of Terror to other Aeldari, but the ordeal led all of them – not least Maugan Ra – to hate Chaos with every fibre of their being. Now, their commitment to the defeat of the Dark Gods and their depraved worshippers quite possibly exceeds that of any other craftworld in the galaxy.

CODEX SUPPLEMENT: ALTANSAR

This section presents the rules for fielding an army formed from Altansar, an Aeldari Craftworld. When choosing a keyword to replace **<CRAFTWORLD>**, you can choose to replace it with **ALTANSAR**. If your army is Battle-forged and includes any **ALTANSAR** units, the rules in this section can be used in addition to those presented in *Codex: Aeldari*.

CRAFTWORLD ATTRIBUTE

The Craftworld Attribute (see *Codex: Aeldari*) gained by Altansar units is Grim Survivors.

ALTANSAR: GRIM SURVIVORS

The Aeldari of Altansar have faced and survived more horrors than most of their kind. The demands placed upon these people have led their craftworld to become heavily militarised, and fighting aboard the world-ship has lent many a penchant for close-quarters combat.

- Each time a model with this attribute makes a melee attack, if that model's unit made a charge move, was charged or performed a Heroic Intervention this turn, improve the Armour Penetration characteristic of that attack by 1.
- Each time a Combat Attrition test is taken for a unit with this attribute, add 1 to that Combat Attrition test.

STRATAGEMS

If your army includes any **ALTANSAR** Detachments (excluding Auxiliary Support, Super-heavy Auxiliary or Fortification Network Detachments), you have access to these Stratagems, and can spend CPs to use them.

INEXHAUSTIBLE HATRED   2CP

Aeldari – Battle Tactic Stratagem

Few Aeldari harbour as much hatred for Chaos in all its guises as those of Altansar. They have seen what horrors it is capable of, and all have experienced great loss to it in one form or another.

Use this Stratagem in the Fight phase, when an **ALTANSAR** unit from your army is selected to fight. Until the end of the phase, each time a model in that unit makes a melee attack against a **DAEMON** unit (excluding **VEHICLE** and **MONSTER** units), add 1 to that attack's wound roll.

DEFIANT TO THE LAST   2CP

Aeldari – Epic Deed Stratagem

The hardship the Altansari have endured for so many millennia has greatly hardened their souls and their bodies. With no safe harbours to flee to in the Eye of Terror and no allies to call upon, they have learnt to hold their ground and fight to the bitter end in order to ensure their survival.

Use this Stratagem at the start of your Command phase. Select one **ALTANSAR** unit from your army. Until the start of your next Command phase, that unit gains the Objective Secured ability (see the Warhammer 40,000 Core Book).

WITHERING VOLLEYS   1CP/2CP

Aeldari – Wargear Stratagem

Maugan Ra's influence has ensured that not only are Altansar's Dark Reapers amongst the finest of their kind but that all warriors of the craftworld are superlative shots. In the fierce fighting that the Altansari have engaged in for millennia, these skills have served them well time and time again.

Use this Stratagem in your Shooting phase, when an **ALTANSAR** unit from your army is selected to shoot. Until the end of the phase, each time a model in that unit makes an attack with an Aeldari missile launcher or Reaper launcher, improve the Armour Penetration characteristic of that attack by 1. If that unit has the **DARK REAPERS** keyword, this Stratagem costs 2CP; otherwise, it costs 1CP.

THRICE-LAYERED WARDS   1CP

Aeldari – Wargear Stratagem

It is a wonder that, after millennia in the Eye of Terror, the Altansari appear to have escaped without being corrupted by the forces of Chaos. Though this is a mystery to a great many Aeldari, what is clear is that the grim craftworlders have hardened their minds to the influence of the warp and have layered many wards onto their armour.

Use this Stratagem in your opponent's Psychic phase, when an **ALTANSAR** unit from your army would suffer a mortal wound. Until the end of the phase, each time a model in that unit would lose a wound, roll one D6: on a 4+, that wound is not lost.

WARLORD TRAITS

If an **Altansar Character** model is your **Warlord**, you can use the Altansar Warlord Traits table below to determine what Warlord Trait they have. You can either roll one D3 to randomly generate one, or you can select one.

1. MASTER OF RUNE-WARDING

This warlord has become a master of suppressing the manifestations and corrupting influence of the warp.

- In your opponent's Psychic phase, if this **Warlord** has the **Psyker** keyword, this **Warlord** can attempt to deny one additional psychic power that phase; otherwise, this **Warlord** can attempt to deny one psychic power that phase as if it were a **Psyker**.
- You can re-roll Deny the Witch tests taken for this **Warlord**.

2. A BEACON OF LIGHT IN THE DARKNESS

This warlord is an inspiring figure to their fellow Altansari, fully committed to the well-being of their people as well as the destruction of their enemies. The warlord's mere presence encourages warriors around to greater feats of courage and to fight harder.

In your Command phase, select one friendly **Altansar** unit within 9" of this **Warlord**. Until the start of your next Command phase:

- If the selected unit is performing an action, it can make ranged attacks without that action failing.
- The selected unit can still perform actions in a turn in which it Advanced or Fell Back.

3. WEAVER OF THE BLADE STORM

This warlord has learnt much from the Altansar schools of thought that emphasise using massed firepower to annihilate the foe, which were formed after countless battles to drive daemons out of the craftworld. As a result, they drill their warriors relentlessly to deliver volley after devastating volley into the enemy.

In your Command phase, select one friendly **Altansar Core** unit within 9" of this **Warlord**. Until the start of your next Command phase, each time a model in the selected unit makes an attack with a shuriken weapon (see *Codex: Aeldari*), an unmodified hit roll of 6 automatically wounds the target.

RELICS

If your army is led by an **Altansar Warlord**, you can, when mustering your army, give one of the following Treasures of the Aeldari Relics to an **Altansar Character** model from your army. Named characters cannot be given any of the following Relics.

Note that some Relics replace one of the model's existing items of wargear. Where this is the case, you must, if you are using points values, still pay the cost of the wargear that is being replaced. Write down any Treasures of the Aeldari Relics your models have on your army roster.

SAVIOUR STONE

This spirit stone holds the soul of one of the Aspect Warriors who was killed fighting beside Maugan Ra to destroy Altansar's webway portals. The warrior's courage and sacrifice serves not only as inspiration to the stone's holder but affords them greater powers of insight into the future. How this is the case many Altansari debate to this day, though it is surmised that the explosive energies unleashed during that fateful battle played a part in infusing the stone with additional power.

At the start of the battle round, when you make a Strands of Fate roll (see *Codex: Aeldari*), if the bearer is on the battlefield, you can do one of the following:

- Increase the result of one of the dice you rolled by 1 (to a maximum of 6).
- Decrease the result of one of the dice you rolled by 1 (to a minimum of 1).

EMBLEM OF THE BROKEN CHAIN

Fashioned by one of Altansar's Bonesingers from part of the Fortress of the Blazing Suns' ruins, this emblem serves to remind its bearer, and other Altansari nearby, that they can survive even the greatest of struggles. Few Aeldari of the craftworld who look upon it and know its story can fail to be emboldened by its symbolism.

In your Command phase, select one friendly **Altansar Core** unit within 6" of the bearer. Until the start of your next Command phase, you can re-roll Advance rolls and charge rolls made for that unit.

CRAFTWORLD ALTANSAR

It's a first for White Dwarf - a painting guide for the Altansar Craftworld! Below you'll find the stages we used to paint a Guardian Windrider, while over the page there's a useful guide to painting the craftworld's symbol and some handy tips for painting gemstones.

The Guardians of Altansar wear deep magenta armour that represents the seas of blood shed by their people in defence of their craftworld. They wear black or bone helms with white faceplates. The bone represents the bones of their ancestors, while the black is symbolic of Maugan Ra, the Phoenix Lord who liberated Altansar from the Eye of Terror.

BATTLE READY

The Windrider was painted in three parts – the jetbike, the rider's body and the rider's helmet. The flying stand was also not glued in place. The jetbike and rider were undercoated with Chaos Black spray, while the helmet was sprayed Wraithbone due to it being a much lighter colour. The majority of the model is one colour, so the rider and

BATTLE READY

Using the stages to the right, this Windrider has been painted to a Battle Ready standard. An army painted to this level would certainly stand out on the table.

PARADE READY

With a few extra highlights to each area of the model, this Guardian has been made Parade Ready. Enemies of Altansar beware!

MAGENTA ARMOUR

1 Basecoat: Gal Vorbak Red & Screamer Pink 1:1
L Base

2 Recess Wash: Basecoat mix & Incubi Darkness 1:1
M Glaze

3 Highlight: Screamer Pink & Evil Sunz Scarlet 1:1
S Layer

4 Highlight: Evil Sunz Scarlet & Ushabti Bone 1:1
XS Artificer Layer

BLACK SEAT

1 Basecoat: Abaddon Black
M Base

2 Highlight: Dawnstone
XS Artificer Layer

JETBIKE SCREEN

1 Basecoat: Kantor Blue
S Base

2 Wash: Abaddon Black & Lahmian Medium
M Glaze

3 Highlight: Calgar Blue
XS Artificer Layer

jetbike were basecoated with a mix of Gal Vorbak Red and Screamer Pink. This Windrider was basecoated by hand with a brush, but if you have access to an airbrush, you can basecoat a lot of models even quicker! Because the magenta tones are all mixes, we recommend mixing up whole pots of the colours you'll need; that way, you'll achieve a consistent colour across your whole army.

The model's helmet was painted bone in this example, though it can also be painted black (a great way to differentiate between units) using the stages for the black seat. Two thin coats of Ushabti Bone were used to build up the colour and ensure even coverage. Just don't be tempted to apply the second layer of paint until the first is thoroughly dry.

PARADE READY

The next stage is to take the model to a Parade Ready standard. When painting the highlights on the armour, paint the first one on quite wide (what we often call a 'chunky' highlight). This means you'll still be able to see it after the final, finer highlight has been applied, providing a better transition of colour.

TOP TIP

When shading the screen between the handlebars, start your brushstroke around three quarters of the way up the screen and draw the brush towards the back of the screen under the canopy. Most of the paint will be deposited at the end of the stroke, making the top section darker. This may require several layers to achieve a smooth colour transition.

JETBIKE ENGINE

Basecoat: Leadbelcher
M Base

Wash: Nuln Oil
M Shade

Highlight: Stormhost Silver
S Layer

BONE ARMOUR

Basecoat: Ushabti Bone
S Base

Recess Wash: Balor Brown
M Glaze

Highlight: Screaming Skull
XS Artificer Layer

WHITE FACEPLATE

Basecoat: Corax White
S Base

Recess Wash: Dawnstone
M Glaze

Highlight: White Scar
XS Artificer Layer

EYE LENSES

Basecoat: Macragge Blue
S Layer

Wash: Nuln Oil
S Layer

Highlight: Calgar Blue
XS Artificer Layer

Highlight: Administratum Grey
XS Artificer Layer

PAINTING THE BROKEN CHAIN

The symbol for Altansar is the Broken Chain, which represents the shattering of the links that bound the Aeldari god Vaul to his anvil. It is often shown on Altansar vehicles, war machines and wraith constructs, either in a prominent position on the upper hull or on the 'head' of the construct. On this Windrider, it is displayed in white on the carapace of the jetbike.

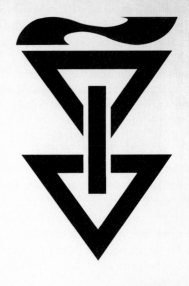

When painting the freehand symbol, it is important to thin the Ulthuan Grey paint and build up the colour gradually. That way you can easily correct any mistakes with the base colour (Gal Vorbak Red and Screamer Pink) rather than trying to paint over a thick grey line! On this model, the main body of the bike was not highlighted until after the freehand design was applied. This makes corrections easier to apply and actually saves time, too. Why bother edge highlighting something when you're going to paint over it with another colour anyway?

To begin with, break down the symbol into simple geometric shapes. In the case of the Broken Chain, the main body of the design is two triangles joined by a thin rectangle. It's useful to have an image of the symbol available for reference at this point!

The first stage is plotting out the corners of the two triangles with dots of Ulthuan Grey (**1**). A tailor's tape measure can help ensure the dots line up over the curved carapace.

Connect the dots with thin lines to make two triangles (**2**).

Fill out the lines of the triangles so they are more solid (**3**).

Add in the vertical line that joins the two triangles (**4**).

Use the basecoat colour mix to help define the three shapes. Paint over the centre of the top triangle at the same time (**5**).

Create the S-shaped rune (**6**). Plot out dots as before, using the symbol below and the lines of the carapace to get the size right. The tails of the rune match the distance between the corner of the triangle and the raised vane along the top of the carapace.

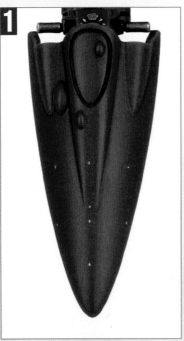

Pink Horror

WARHAMMER

Need a little extra magenta in your life? Then check out the 'Craftworld Altansar Armour' painting video on our Warhammer YouTube channel. There are loads of other easy-to-follow guides on there for Aeldari, too, including alternative craftworld colour schemes and how to paint witchblades, Dire Avengers and Howling Banshees. There are also videos for gemstones, wraithbone, eye lenses, pale skin, and countless other useful things. You'll have your Aeldari painted in no time.

SPIRIT STONES

Every Craftworld Aeldari wears at least one spirit stone about their person, most commonly mounted on their armour above their heart. It's these tiny gems that capture their soul when they die, saving it from the predations of She Who Thirsts. Aspect Warriors, wraith constructs and vehicles may feature multiple spirit stones on their armour, which help channel the power, energy and wisdom of former warriors, seers and pilots.

There are no rules for what colour spirit stones should be. However, often people tend to paint them in a colour that contrasts with the primary colour of their craftworld. For example, most people paint the spirit stones for Ulthwé red to contrast with the black armour, while blue is a common choice next to the yellow armour of Iyanden. For the warriors of Altansar, a bright cyan or green would work well. You could even use the colours for the eye lenses shown on the previous page.

A useful thing to note: spirit stones always have a 'mount' or surround. In the pictures to the right, the spirit stone is in the centre; the bulbs on either side are part of the armour.

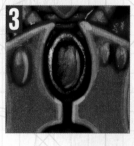

Apply your basecoat over the whole spirit stone **(1)**. Here we used Caliban Green.

Apply a lighter layer of colour diagonally across the bottom half of the gem **(2)**. We used Warpstone Glow. Most right-handed people tend to paint this lighter colour on the right, and most left-handed people do it on the left. Both are fine!

Apply a highlight just around the bottom curve of the gem **(3)**. Here we used Moot Green.

Place a tiny dot of White Scar in the top corner opposite the highlight to represent a light reflection point **(4)**.

Apply a layer of 'Ardcoat to achieve a shiny finish **(5)**.

TOP TIP

Try using the Technical 'gemstone' paints to create quick and effective spirit stones. Simply paint them straight over a bright gold or silver basecoat for great results!

LOYALISTS AND RENEGADES

Welcome to our first Readers' Gallery - a place where we show off some of the very best miniatures painted by you, our readers! For this inaugural article, we delved deep into the team inbox to bring you an impressive selection of Imperial and Chaos Knights. Enjoy!

KNIGHT DESECRATOR BY DANIEL JACKSON

Daniel: Knight Desecrator Hashin belongs to House K'Thruul, a long-term ally of the Dark Mechanicum. K'Thruul welcomes Renegade Knights no matter their past, so long as they subject themselves to the rule of the dark priesthood. When it came to painting him, I used glazes to subtly change the colour gradient in his carapace from a dark grey to green. The idea was to show that the Knight has been slowly corrupted, the daemonic energy working its way from the pilot and generator into the livery. The skull logo on his banner and shield represent the house's view that the infernal relationship between the immaterium and the machine can overcome death.

KYTAN DAEMON ENGINE BY RAFAEL MATTICK

Rafael: The Kytan is an aggressive Daemon Engine, so I posed it striding forward with its upper torso leaning in to the attack. The right hand with the axe raised high is ready to strike, while the left hand is tilted downwards to emphasise the dynamic pose. I primed the model black before spraying the head, arms, torso and the armour plates on the legs from above with Mephiston Red. I then glazed the surface with black to create a gradient and highlighted the edges with Wild Rider Red. A few battlescars picked out with black and metal complete the effect. The bronze trim was washed with Agrax Earthshade, which I worked heavily into the recesses. Nihilakh Oxide was used for the oxidisation. I added object source lighting around the eyes and heat vents to bring the piece to life.

KNIGHT ERRANT OF HOUSE HAWKSHROUD BY VIET NGUYEN

Viet: Sir Scrugg, pilot of Xenobane, has dedicated his life to defending Mankind against the horrors of the galaxy. His Knight Errant earned its name on the world of Olympus IV after holding the line against a swarm of Tyranids from Hive Fleet Jormungandr. He single-handedly killed a Hierophant bio-titan before charging the Hive Tyrant and slaying it in combat. Xenobane was left immobilized and without ammo, facing down a brood of Carnifexes. However, with the loss of the synaptic link to the Hive Mind, the swarm was broken by an armoured spearhead assault from Astra Militarum forces of the 20th Lazarian Storm. A squadron of Leman Russ Battle Tanks annihilated the Carnifex brood, sparing Xenobane a brutal death.

Decades later, when the verdant world of Lazaria came under attack by Necrons, the now Baron Scrugg came to their aid to repay his debt. The conflict has dragged on for half a decade, but Baron Scrugg has vowed to see the conflict through to the end alongside the Lazarians and their allies from House Taranis and the Legio Ignatum.

I painted my Knight using an airbrush. The Citadel colours for the yellow armour are Mournfang Brown, Yriel Yellow and Flash Gitz Yellow. I then used The Fang, Russ Grey and White Scar for the white panels. The metal is shaded with Guilliman Blue to give the slight blue effect.

DREADBLADE KNIGHT BY DAMIAN KOBIALKA

Damian: Sanguine Propheta is a Dreadblade piloted by Sander Malakhai. The Knight comes from a fallen minor house that was based on a world at the edge of the Ghoul Stars. When a loyalist Chapter of Adeptus Astartes purged the planet on suspicion of heresy, those nobles who escaped the cull took their machines and pledged allegiance to the Dark Gods, seeking revenge.

I wanted to create a contrast between the Knight and the rest of my Chaos army (Night Lords), so instead of dark colours I choose something brighter, and instead of wild and chaotic lightning motifs I chose something more

structured and geometric. I used basic shapes for the heraldry. To make both the stripes and chequered patterns, I used masking tape. I cut it down into thin strips, which I placed on the armour panels (for the diamond pattern, I removed the strips after the first layer of paint, then placed new strips at 90° to the initial ones). When I had them ready, I blocked in my chosen colours and then highlighted them. At the very end, I added another simple yet striking detail to the model: an eye on a banner. On one hand, it's an obvious call to the Horus Heresy. On the other, it creates a point of interest on the model and complements the overall knightly-yet-fallen theme.

IMPERIAL KNIGHT CRUSADER BY DAMIEN TOMASINA

Damien: This Imperial Crusader is a Freeblade, previously from House Drakkus. Having recently joined the Iron Warden of Tarnis, he helped reconquer Tarnis alongside the Dark Angels, with whom he shares an alliance.

Symbols of this alliance can be seen everywhere on the Knight's armour: the Sword of Revenge (shown on the carapace and greave), the robed monk and the deployed wing icon of the Dark Angels share space with the Imperial Eagle. I also used Caliban Green as one of the two main armour colours, marrying it with violet to symbolise mourning – a reminder that House Drakkus is no more. However, the Knight continues to fight for them still.

I painted the armour trim in polished blue steel using a non-metallic metal technique to give me better control of the reflection points. This choice also enabled me to create a reflective sky-earth effect on the cannons. I painted a black section along the bottom of the guns to represent the horizon. I then added a light area above it to represent the rising sun. This fades back into the blue steel colour of the metalwork.

I finished the guns by adding brown and black to the tips of the cannons to show they have been well used. I also added rust, dust and streaks of oil to the Knight to show the effects of the environment on its armour.

KNIGHT RAMPAGER BY KENNETH TAN

Kenneth: When painting my Chaos Knight, I drew a lot of inspiration from the artwork. There's an illustration of Decima, Incarnate Slaughter, which has a really dynamic pose that I decided to emulate on the model. I cut the limbs at the joints and reposed them using brass rods to reinforce them and allow the model to stand on one foot.

For the painting, I wanted to replicate the dusty, textured effect in the artwork. I stippled on thinned-down paints to create a mottled effect on the armour panels and then added weathering pigments to make the Knight look aged. As scale modellers often place a lot of emphasis on different types of metal, I decided to show the different materials the Knight is made from through the weathering. I added blue verdigris to the copper areas and brown rust to the iron components. In some places, you can see where the painted armour has been chipped away to reveal bare metal that has now also begun to rust.

IMPERIAL KNIGHT WARDEN BY MICHAEL AUSTIN COYNE

Michael: This is Baron Hector of the Crimson Rose House. Deeply pious warriors of the Imperial Creed, the house's keep can be found on a shrine world, for they have strong connections with the Ecclesiarchy. They can often be found on crusade, purging heretics, protecting pilgrim fleets or guarding the gates of temples.

The Imperial Knight kit is versatile, and, with some neat cutting of the joints, you can get a some very dynamic poses. I positioned my Knight's leg to be standing on ruins, his thunderstrike gauntlet pointing a challenge at an unseen foe. For painting, I kept the 'skeleton' and armour plates separate. Starting with a Mournfang Brown basecoat, I drybrushed the skeleton Leadbelcher and then added a mix of a brown and black wash over the whole thing. I finished it off by drybrushing and sponging it with silver. The black and white armour was masked off with tape and then sprayed using black and white undercoat sprays.

KNIGHT CASTELLAN OF HOUSE TERRYN BY STEVEN GARCIA

Steve: Hail Fury's Glory, Knight Castellan of House Terryn, piloted by Lord Georgen, Warden of the Rock (named after our Warhammer store manager).

The most notable features on the Knight are his finely crafted marble armour, known as Heaven's Aegis, and his legendary plasma decimator, Emperor's Kiss. The marble plating was achieved by sponging shades of grey and white on top of the black primer, after which I added random white veins with a detail brush. Once dry, I applied thinned Contrast paints in multiple layers until the desired colour intensity was met.

Ultramarines Blue, Blood Angels Red and a 1:1 mix of Basilicanum Grey and Black Templar were used on the different areas over the greyscale marble effect. Decals and freehand details were then applied. With this method, light-coloured decals allow the marbling effect to show through really well. Finally, a layer of gloss varnish was applied to seal it all together. The rest of the blue armour plates were basecoated with Kantor Blue and highlighted with a mix of Macragge Blue and Sotek Green. I added Lothern Blue to the mix for further highlights before applying a final highlight of Teclis Blue.

SEND US YOUR PICTURES!
We are always looking for beautifully painted miniatures to feature in the pages of *White Dwarf*. If you think your models have what it takes to appear in a Readers' Gallery, send us some high-quality pics to:

team@ whitedwarf.co.uk

JOHN BRACKEN

As one of the writers on Warhammer Underworlds, John Bracken is the man responsible for bringing you the game's many rich and varied settings, including this season's Harrowdeep. Oppressively gloomy, violently mercurial and emanating a disquieting aura of sinister malevolence, John is a games developer in the Age of Sigmar Studio.

F ollowing hot on the heels of Fatal Edge (presented in issue 470), I'm bringing you yet another new and exciting play variant for Warhammer Underworlds. **The rules presented here are intended to provide you with different challenges and experiences in a twist to the familiar game.**

So, destroy your enemies and cast down the mighty as you lose your fighters to feral instincts deep within the twisting corridors of Harrowdeep.

THE UNTAMED RELICS

In dread Harrowdeep, deep beneath the ocean, the walls tremble. Whether this occurrence is purely magical in nature – perhaps a wide-ranging effect of Ghur's anger – or the result of the predatory aspect of Harrowdeep's umbral creators being pushed to the surface is unknown. What is beyond doubt is the effect being had on those magical items hidden within the labyrinth's maddening halls.

Savage and primal magic surges through the walls, seeping into all who walk those darksome corridors. Worse affected of all are those potent relics of Harrowdeep in which magical energies naturally

pool, ordinarily giving birth to powerful arcane items. Normally objects of extreme value, these treasures had a wide variety of uses, from providing clues on how to escape Harrowdeep, no matter how obfuscated, to siphoning arcane power from the shadows, to name but a few. Now, however, such subtle uses and clever tricks are gone, replaced by an all-consuming desire to hunt and gather. Once a fighter but lays their hands on these Untamed Relics, their every thought is turned to the hunt, and only after they lie panting and blood-soaked on a veritable hoard of these artefacts does their sanity return.

HOW TO PLAY

To play a game of Untamed Relics, use all of the rules presented in your Warhammer Underworlds Core Set with the following changes. Where a rule presented here contradicts a rule in your Warhammer Underworlds Core Set, use the rule presented here.

OBJECTIVE

The objective of a game of Untamed Relics is to have more glory points than your opponent at the end of the game.

PLAYING THE GAME

To play a game of Untamed Relics between two players, set up and play through a game of Warhammer Underworlds using the rules from the rulebook with the following changes. To play Untamed Relics with three or more players, use these rules with the additions under 'Multiplayer Rules' later.

PLACE THE BOARDS

The players roll off. The player who wins picks a player. The player they pick chooses a game board from their collection and decides which side of that game board they will use as their territory. The other player then chooses a game board and a side in the same way and places those boards in such a way that the two boards are in one of the two following positions.

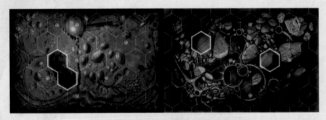

The first player to pick their board now chooses another board and places it so that it is in either of the two following positions.

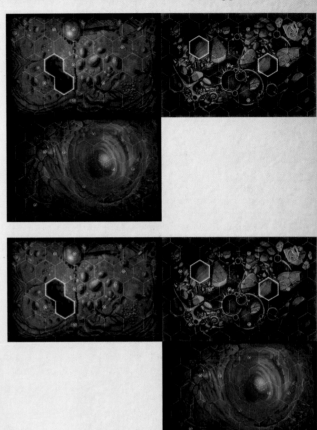

Finally, the other player places their second board in the remaining available position, leaving the battlefield appearing as follows.

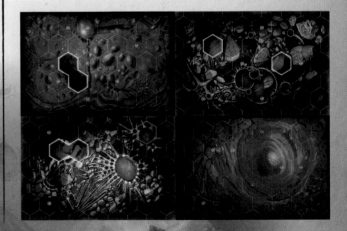

TERRITORIES

In games of Untamed Relics, a player's territory is made up of all the hexes on their game boards. Hexes on the other player's game boards are enemy territory. Hexes completed by the placement of two game boards chosen by the same player are included in that player's territory. Other hexes completed by the placement of game boards are no one's territory. This means that it is possible for the territories of each player to be in any of the following formations.

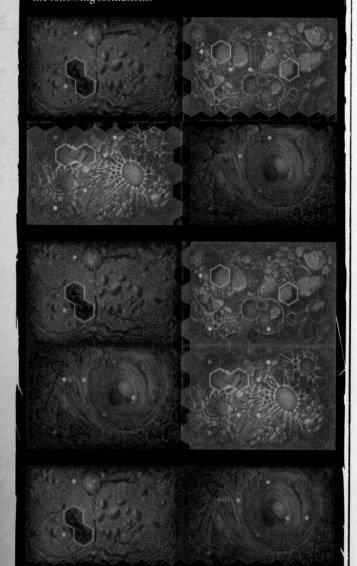

Once all four game boards are placed, you have what is called the battlefield.

PLACE FEATURE TOKENS

Follow these rules instead of the ones presented in the Warhammer Underworlds rules.

Use feature tokens to represent Untamed Relics. Untamed Relic tokens are not feature tokens.

Place one Untamed Relic token in the centremost hex of each game board.

UNTAMED RELICS

The following rules apply to Untamed Relic tokens.

Each time a fighter is placed, moved, or pushed into a hex that contains one or more Untamed Relic tokens, that fighter is given those Untamed Relics. Place the Untamed Relics next to that fighter's fighter card to remind you.

While a fighter has one or more Untamed Relics, they are Untamed. The following rules apply to Untamed fighters.

- An Untamed fighter's Move characteristic is 5.

- An Untamed fighter's Defence characteristic is 1 🛡.

- An Untamed fighter's Wounds characteristic is 4.

- An Untamed fighter's Move, Defence and Wounds characteristics cannot be modified further.

- +1 Dice to an Untamed fighter's Range 1 Attack actions.

When an Untamed fighter's Attack action or spell takes an enemy fighter out of action, the bounty for that enemy fighter is worth additional glory points equal to the number of Untamed Relics the attacking fighter has.

When an Untamed fighter is taken out of action, place each of their Untamed Relics in the hex that Untamed fighter occupied before they were taken out of action.

VICTORY

Whichever player has the highest number of glory points at the end of round 3 is the winner. If the players are tied for the highest number of points, the winner is the player with fighters still on the battlefield. If there are still fighters from both warbands on the battlefield, whichever player has the most Untamed fighters is the winner. If there is still a tie, the player whose fighters have the most Untamed Relics is the winner. If there is still a tie, the game is a draw.

MULTIPLAYER GAMES

You can play Untamed Relics with three or four players. For the most part, you will follow all of the rules for a multiplayer game of Warhammer Underworlds, using the changes where appropriate for a two-player game of Untamed Relics, but there are some significant additional changes to the Untamed Relic rules, which are detailed here.

PLACE THE BOARDS

The players roll off. Whoever loses chooses a game board and a side of that game board to use. This can be any board from their collection. The remaining players roll off again, and the loser chooses a game board and side next, then places it adjacent to the first board and in one of the positions shown below.

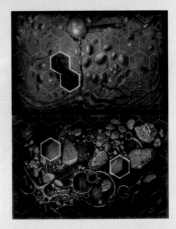

If there are two players left, they roll off again and the player who scores lowest does the same, placing their board adjacent to at least one of the boards already placed so that the final formation of boards appears as below.

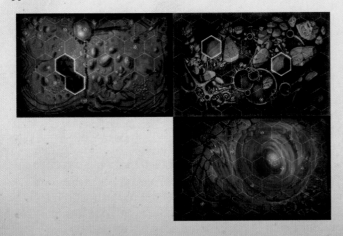

If there are no more players, the first player chooses a game board and a side in the same way and places that board in such a way that the four boards are in the following position. Otherwise this is done by the fourth player.

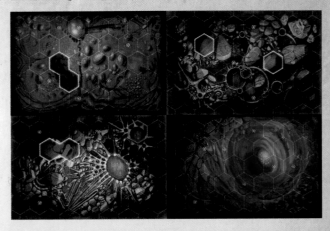

Once all four game boards are placed, you have what is called the battlefield.

VICTORY

Whichever player has the highest number of glory points at the end of round 3 is the winner. If two or more players are tied for the highest number of points, the winner is the tied player with fighters still on the battlefield. If there are still fighters from more than one of these warbands on the battlefield, whichever tied player has the most Untamed fighters is the winner. If there is still a tie, the player whose fighters have the most Untamed Relics is the winner. If there is still a tie, the game is a draw between those players.

END PHASE

There is nothing quite like a usually slow or even fragile fighter turning into a ravening hungry beast that wants to track down others like it and tear them apart with their bare hands. The thought of a weedy grot turning into a frothing, super-fast, pint-sized killing machine (okay, I'm exaggerating just a little here) is both endearing and hilarious in equal measure. I hope you enjoy tramping around a much bigger arena and clobbering anyone who gets in your way as much as I enjoyed putting the idea down on paper.

TELL US YOUR THOUGHTS

Write us if you have any suggestions or something that you'd like to read about. You can contact us at:

whunderworlds@gwplc.com

or by sending a letter to John Bracken, Books and Box Games, Games Workshop, Willow Road, Nottingham, NG7 2WS.

HONOUR BANNERS

The god-engines of the Collegia Titanica have illustrious histories, many stretching back thousands of years. These impressive sagas are often recorded on honour banners. Here we show how to keep a log of your own Titans' feats and create your own Titan banners.

Titans of the Collegia Titanica are often depicted with honour banners. Each one is a chronicle of the god-engine's achievements since its forging, depicting its glorious deeds on battlefields across the galaxy. If you've ever looked at a piece of Titan artwork and wondered what it all means, this is the article for you! Within, we'll explore the different elements that make up an honour banner, as well as how Titan Legios vary when crafting their honour banners. We'll also give some guidance on how to track the deeds of your own Titans, with the aim of creating an honour banner for each.

HONOUR, WHAT ART THOU?

Honour banners have been used since the creation of the first three Titan Legios – together known as the *Triad Ferrum Morgulus* – during the Age of Strife. Each banner is resplendent with detail and serves as a record of a Titan's origins, honours and battlefield kills. This record was continually added to, even during the dark days of the

Horus Heresy. The principles for honour banners have remained largely consistent across Titan Legios, though many have their own minor divergent practices.

Honour banners are most commonly worn when a Titan is mustering for battle or deployed as part of a triumphal march, and they are traditionally worn between the Titan's legs. It is less common for a god-engine to enter battle adorned with such ceremonial honour banners, as the cataclysmic nature of any campaign involving the Collegia Titanica will often see such treasured relics reduced to charred ruin. To prevent the complete destruction of a god-engine's legacy during battle, each Titan has multiple honour banners. The honour banners carried by a battlegroup are personally maintained by the Titans' crew and updated whenever the tide of war allows.

At least one of these copies is stored on the Forge World of origin within the Titan Legio's vaults and updated periodically when news of a god-engine's victories and honours reaches the planet. This task is handled by cadres of blessed scriveners who meticulously inscribe new details while excising and preserving outdated elements such as old maniple configurations. During the Horus Heresy, some excised parts would be destroyed if they referenced those who fought for the opposing side.

Smaller honour banners can often be seen hanging from a Titan's weapons. These are the kills ascribed to the individual weapon and attributed to the Moderati who controls it. If a Moderati perishes, their honour banner is returned in full honour to the Forge World, and a new one is commissioned for the new Moderati.

To better understand honour banners and to get insight into creating your own, it's best to take a look at some examples and the different elements of them.

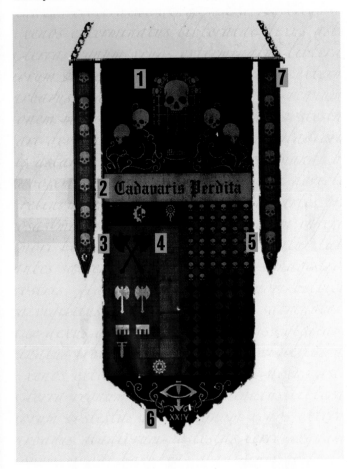

This honour banner is from the Legio Mortis Warlord Battle Titan *Cadavaris Perdita*, as it was depicted shortly before the battle for Prospero in 004.M31. It shares the common elements of most honour banners, and it showcases some deviations associated with Legio Mortis.

1. **Legio Heraldry** – The Legio's heraldry takes pride of place on most honour banners, sitting above the god-engine's deeds in recognition that all is done in service to its Titan Legio.

2. **Titan Name** – The god-engine's name. Sometimes replaced with the name of the Titan's Forge World, its maniple name or similar descriptor.

3. **Maniple Disposition** – A symbolic breakdown of the god-engines within the Titan's maniple. Each symbol represents a class of Titan, with a different colour (in this case black) used to denote the honour banner's owner.

4. **Litany of Deeds** – Text is commonplace on honour banners, often describing the Titan's forging and/or its most memorable victories and accomplishments. Each word is hand-painted using emulsions mixed with thrice-blessed oils.

5. **Kill Markings** – A tally of the Titan's kills. These represent Titan analogue targets rather than lesser foes such as infantry or most tanks. Skulls (as seen here) are the most common markings used, but there are many variations. One common practice is the use of Titan class icons, to denote foes of similar scale to the respective classes or, during the Horus Heresy, to display the type of enemy Titans the god-engine had slain.

6. **Lauded Honours** – A common practice is the presence of honours bestowed upon a Titan by its Legio or by external agencies. In this case, *Cadavaris Perdita* bears the Eye of Horus in recognition of its long service in the 63rd Expeditionary Fleet to the Warmaster's cause.

7. **Notable Foes** – Legio Mortis Titans often use periphery banners that detail the most notable kills, rendered with larger symbols, and a short passage on the relevant engagement.

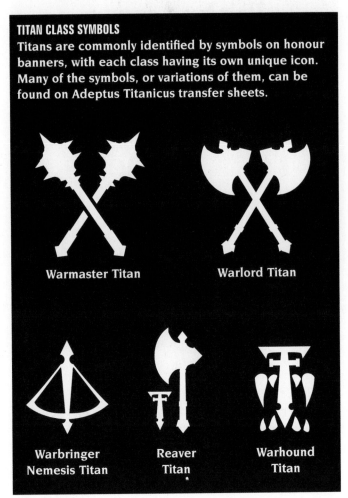

TITAN CLASS SYMBOLS
Titans are commonly identified by symbols on honour banners, with each class having its own unique icon. Many of the symbols, or variations of them, can be found on Adeptus Titanicus transfer sheets.

Warmaster Titan

Warlord Titan

Warbringer Nemesis Titan

Reaver Titan

Warhound Titan

CRAFTING YOUR OWN HONOUR BANNERS

Armed with the preceding knowledge, you can now create honour banners for your own Titans for Adeptus Titanicus (and Warhammer 40,000 and Horus Heresy: The Age of Darkness, if you wish). To represent a snapshot of the Titan's honours during the time of the Horus Heresy, you can design a banner incorporating whichever elements you like, combining them to create your own narrative.

A more interactive approach is to track each Titan's achievements over the course of an Adeptus Titanicus campaign (rules for which can be found in the *Titandeath* and *Shadow* and *Iron* supplements). This can be done through a campaign journal where you note down kills and mighty deeds for each of your Titans.

The following pages provide examples of how to keep a campaign journal. When doing so, note down when a Titan

destroys an enemy god-engine — additional details, such as the weapon that struck the blow and/or the class of the destroyed Titan can also be included. You can also use gridded paper to draw a mock honour banner that you update, which will aid you in creating a physical banner later. Over the course of a campaign, a Titan's honour banner will grow more illustrious, and, by creating a physical banner, you'll forever be displaying the god-engine's legacy in every game to come!

YOUR OWN LEGIO

This article provides a guide for designing your own honour banners, but don't feel you have to stick rigidly to the symbols seen in existing artwork. There were dozens upon dozens of Titan Legios, each with their own customs. We've included some additional examples showing variant honour banners below to inspire you when creating your own.

A **Legio Gryphonicus** honour banner belonging to the Reaver *Paladin Argentus*. The War Griffons use chess pieces to denote Titan class: the King for a Warmaster, the Queen for a Warlord, the Bishop for a Warbringer, the Knight for a Reaver and the Pawn for a Warhound.

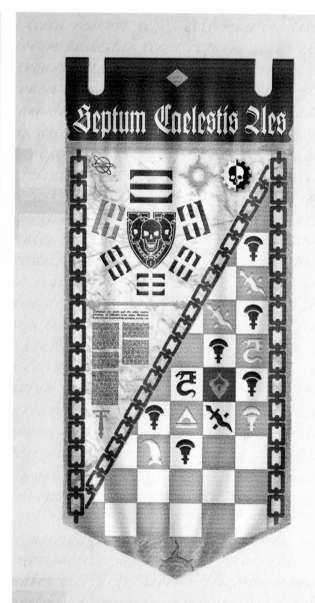

A **Legio Xestobiax** Reaver Titan honour banner belonging to *Septum Caelestis Des*. The Iron Vigil used ideographs as kill markings that reflected the species or threat in question. Unique Titan class icons are also present, denoting Warlord and Reaver Titans.

CAMPAIGN JOURNAL

A reliable method for keeping track of your Legio's victories and Titan honours is a campaign journal. A campaign journal is a narrative tool that can be combined with the campaign roster found in *Titandeath* (pg 85) and *Shadow and Iron* (pg 79).

Each campaign journal should contain a Titan log for each Titan in the battleforce and a collection of battle logs, each recounting the noteworthy battles in which they have fought. An example battle log is shown to the right.

Each battle log should list the name (**1**) and date (**2**) of the battle, plus your Titan Legio (**3**) and your opponent's Titan Legio (**4**). It also offers a spot to name your battlegroup (**5**).

Total engine kills is where you list the total number of enemy Titans killed (**6**). You'll list them individually on the relevant Titan logs.

Include your Primary objective (**7**) and any Secondary objectives (**8**) that you had during the battle.

Record under outcome whether the battle was a win, a loss or a draw (**9**) for your Titan Legio.

The notes section (**10**) is where you write about anything noteworthy. This can include interesting battle conditions (such as battling during a meteor shower), moments of extreme heroism, fun occurrences and anything else that strikes your fancy. It pays to note down which of your Titans scored engine kills along with the weapon that struck the final blow and the enemy Titan destroyed; this will help you with Titan logs later.

TITAN LOGS

Each Titan should have its own log page in a campaign journal. You can use this to track the individual honour markings of each Titan. An example log is shown to the right.

Each Titan journal should include the Titan's name (**11**), its class (**12**) and the Legio it is from (**13**). If you wish, you can also name its Princeps (**14**) and any Moderatii (in general, a Titan will have one Moderati per weapon) (**15**) as well as the date it first walked from the forges (**16**). Most Titans fighting during the Heresy were created during the Age of Strife (*ca.* M25-M30) so a date from sometime during this period is particularly appropriate.

The conflict record (**17**) is a chronicle of the battles the Titan has fought in. This will be the games played during the campaign, with notes on anything particularly inspiring they did.

An example entry might be:
Battled Legio Infernus on the burning sands of Naldor VI. Laid low two traitorous Warhounds before participating in a tactical withdrawal.

Engine kills (**18**) is where you expand upon the Titan's kills. Include the class of each slain Titan, the Legio it was from and, if appropriate, the weapon that was used to slay it.

The engine kills section can then be used to populate your honour banner (see the next page) (**19**); for each kill, fill in a square on the banner's kill markings tally. As previously noted, this can be done with skulls, Titan class symbols or other icons.

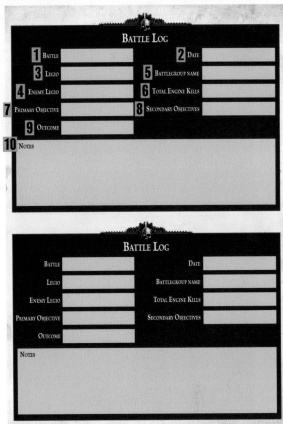

BATTLE LOG

1 Battle	**2** Date
3 Legio	**5** Battlegroup name
4 Enemy Legio	**6** Total Engine Kills
7 Primary Objective	**8** Secondary Objectives
9 Outcome	
10 Notes	

BATTLE LOG

Battle	Date
Legio	Battlegroup name
Enemy Legio	Total Engine Kills
Primary Objective	Secondary Objectives
Outcome	
Notes	

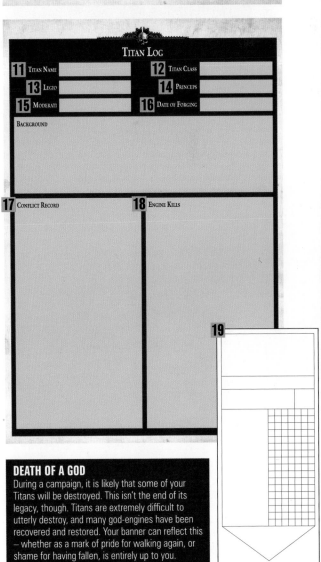

TITAN LOG

11 Titan Name	**12** Titan Class
13 Legio	**14** Princeps
15 Moderati	**16** Date of Forging
Background	

17 Conflict Record	**18** Engine Kills

19

DEATH OF A GOD
During a campaign, it is likely that some of your Titans will be destroyed. This isn't the end of its legacy, though. Titans are extremely difficult to utterly destroy, and many god-engines have been recovered and restored. Your banner can reflect this — whether as a mark of pride for walking again, or shame for having fallen, is entirely up to you.

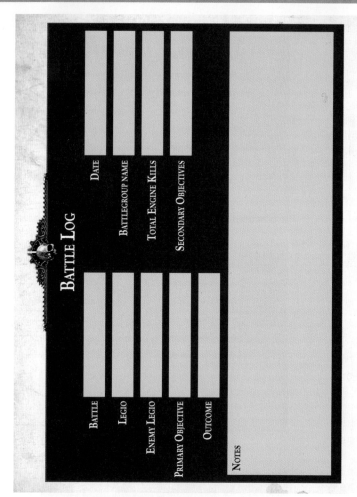

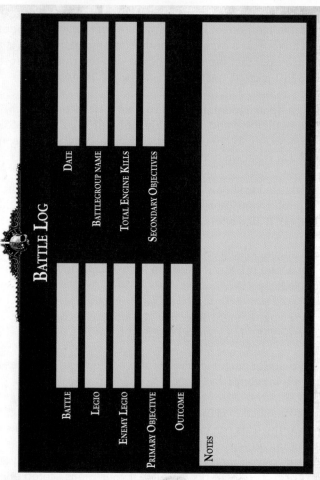

BATTLE LOG

Date

Battlegroup Name

Total Engine Kills

Secondary Objectives

Battle

Legio

Enemy Legio

Primary Objective

Outcome

Notes

We recommend using an A5 journal to create your own campaign journal. Photocopy and insert the pages on these spreads into your journal, or use a gridded or dotted journal to replicate these pages. You will need one Titan Log and Titan Banner page for each of the Titans in your collection, plus a Battle Log entry for each game you play. You can photocopy the small banners to the right to recreate your Titans' honour banners in miniature scale, perfect for adorning your models.

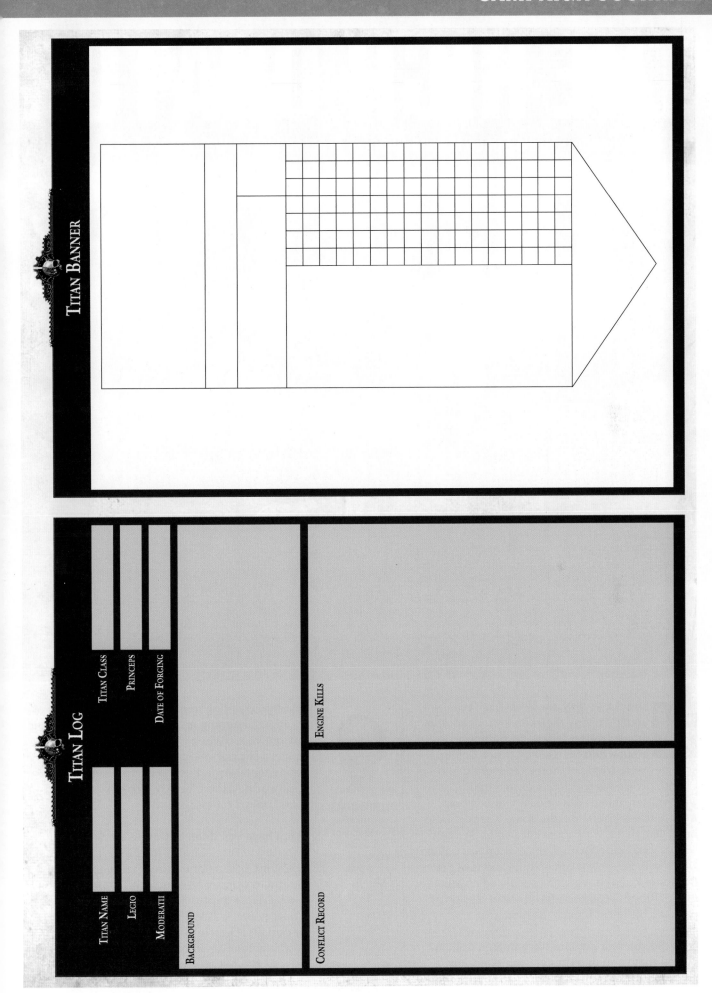

TITAN BANNER

TITAN LOG

TITAN NAME

LEGIO

MODERATII

TITAN CLASS

PRINCEPS

DATE OF FORGING

BACKGROUND

CONFLICT RECORD

ENGINE KILLS

THE HIGH ORATOR

The Tome Keepers are a Space Marine Chapter created by the White Dwarf team and now immortalised in literary form by a six-part Black Library serial. Author Callum Davis joins us to talk about creating legends, writing tomes and introducing a suitably devious foe.

Way back in 2019, the *White Dwarf* team set about creating their very own Chapter of Space Marines. Ideas were thrown around and then nailed down. Colour schemes were tried out, heroes converted and Chapter icons designed. Stories and traditions were written, names devised and heroes born. After much deliberation, the Tome Keepers were born. One of the Warhammer 40,000 background writers who helped with their creation was Callum Davis, who has now taken up quill and ink to pen the Tome Keepers' very first serialised novella for Black Library. We asked him all about his hobby past and his latest literary creation.

How did you first get into Warhammer, Callum?
I recall that someone brought some models to school in their lunch box. I knew it was my thing the moment I saw them. Since then, I've always been involved in the hobby in some way,

CALLUM DAVIS
Callum works in the Warhammer 40,000 Studio as a background writer, but in previous incarnations, he worked in the Black Library and Forge World editorial teams. Now he has lent his talents to Black Library once more to write this awesome Tome Keepers serial.

whether painting miniatures, reading novels or even just keeping an eye on the website during my uni years. When I joined Games Workshop, it was a slippery slope into total hobby immersion. My largest collection is my Craftworld Aeldari force, which sits at around 7,000 points (at last count!).

What have you done at Games Workshop?
I started in Black Library in 2015 as an editorial assistant. I then joined the Specialist Design Studio to work as an editor on *The Horus Heresy: Malevolence*, Adeptus Titanicus, the Middle-earth Strategy Battle Game and Aeronautica Imperialis. Then in 2018, I moved into the Warhammer 40,000 team as a background writer. A lot of my first articles and stories were the ones published in *White Dwarf*, but I've also worked on a number of codexes, including Space Marines, Blood Angels and Death Guard,

along with the Octarius books, Psychic Awakening and the recent Chalnath book for Kill Team.

How did you get the Tome Keepers gig?

Black Library had just commissioned the Grombrindal serial, and White Dwarf wanted one for Warhammer 40,000 based on something unique to the magazine. The Tome Keepers were the perfect choice. They thought I'd be a good fit for the job because I was involved in the discussions for the 'Creation of a Chapter' articles. We thought it would be cool to expand upon the characters presented in the Index Astartes article (issue 458 – Ed).

So what's the story about?

It's actually a series of six individual stories linked together by a common thread. The first story presented in issue 472 sees the 3rd Company stuck in a protracted war with the necrons in the Pariah Nexus. Having written a fair chunk of the Pariah Nexus background for White Dwarf, I knew the Tome Keepers wouldn't be the deciding factor in that campaign, and these stories didn't seem to be the right place to conclude that narrative either. So Will Moss – he's the commissioning editor in Black Library – and I decided they needed a new mission and a new foe. If you read the previous instalment, you'll know that Captain Nasiem – frustrated with the grinding war of attrition on Foronika – withdraws his company to deal with an insurrection on the shrine world of Anakletos, an important link in the supply chain of the crusade fleet. This is the sort of mission that Space Marines excel at – a swift, decisive strike executed with brutal efficiency. But, of course, things don't go to plan!

Who are they fighting now?

That was one of our first questions. The Tome Keepers pride themselves on knowing their foe and using past experiences and tactics to defeat them. They always study for their exams! But what if the enemy is cleverer than they are? We thought it would be interesting to introduce a foe that could run rings around them and leave them guessing, stirring up threats they'll struggle to deal with and making a mockery of their best-laid plans. I won't give the game away and say who the big bad is, but the main antagonists will be revealed to the reader about halfway through the series. The Tome Keepers won't realise their plight until closer towards the end.

What was it like writing about them?

The stories actually ended up becoming quite personal. There are still plenty of guns and lots of action throughout the serial, but I really enjoyed delving into the characters and the culture of the Chapter. The Index Astartes article was a great starting point, giving me lots of ideas to work with and explore. I spent a fair amount of time wondering what it takes to become a Tome Keeper. They are warriors and scholars combined, so it felt only right to introduce some literary feats into the Trial of Pages, like reading scriptures after climbing a mountain, or lifting a huge book clad in the heaviest metal known to man before reading crucial passages from it. Tapping into the history of the Chapter was key as they recount it all the time. I had to know and understand that history before I could write

about it in allegory, which is how the battle-brothers often talk about it, be it as a way to convey their tactics or just in passing conversation. They refer to events easily and casually – it is a shared knowledge and understanding. So when one speaks of the seventh rotation of such-and-such, it means there are at least seven ways to do something that only this brotherhood really understands. There's a level of depth and complexity to their tactics that is absolutely fascinating for a writer.

I also really loved writing about the four main characters mentioned in the Index: Nasiem, Kae, Lykandos and Sephax. The six stories revolve around them, with each becoming a focal character in their own story. This allowed me to explore them from their own point of view as well as those of their battle-brothers. They are all part of the company command hierarchy, yet they are all individuals, too. Nasiem and Kae know each other, but the Librarian and Orator are Greyshields and still relatively new to the Chapter. It was interesting exploring that and their approach to warfare. Sephax is bellicose and wants to hit things with his mace until the job is done. He has a blunt way of doing things. Lykandos is more in favour of caution, care and thought. The two clash in their views somewhat, and the fighting in the Argovon sector strains that even further. Kae sits somewhere between the two in his views, while Nasiem has to deal with a lot of inner turmoil. He's a very introspective character for a Space Marine, which was really interesting to explore. In many ways he's human, but he's also both more and less than human at the same time. That must be tough to deal with.

Do you have a favourite character?

Ooh, tough. I would be tempted to say Sephax. He is very straightforward, but his views and opinions change quite a lot over the course of the series. He doesn't initially understand the importance of the personal tomes the battle-brothers carry, but in an upcoming part of the serial, when he reads one owned by a deceased Greyshield and finds it virtually empty, he begins to understand. He knew the battle-brother and the valiant feats he had achieved in battle, his skill and bravery, and the odds he fought against. Yet now there is no memory of him or his achievements. So little to remember him by. That really strikes a chord with the Orator. But you've got a while to go before you read that story! In the meantime, turn the page and enjoy the second instalment: Duel of Words.

DUEL OF WORDS

By Callum Davis

Anarchy reigns in the skies above Anakletos as insurrection threatens supply lines vital to the Indomitus Crusade. As the Tome Keepers make planetfall, old grievances raise their heads, and it appears that they will find few allies in the second part of Heirs of Reason.

The sight that greeted the Tome Keepers' fleet as it entered Anakletos's space was one of total disorder. Thousands of vessels flocked in and around the troubled world's orbit: warships, troop transports, merchant vessels, pleasure yachts, industrial tugs, fighter squadrons, and countless others. Many were on fire, leaking fluids or severely damaged and were barely held together by patchwork repairs. There were enormous debris fields made up of the shattered remains of human and alien ships, each obscuring the view from the *Hariwok* as well as making any kind of weapons' targeting all but impossible, should that be needed.

Swarms of drop-ships moved between the surface and the crowd of vessels or between the vessels themselves, all packed with refugees, supplies, troops or repair crews. Ecclesiarchal auxiliary patrol boats flitted around the shoals of voidcraft, attempting to force order to a situation that bordered on total anarchy. Damaged ships jostled for position to dock with a handful of orbital stations that resembled the unfortunate victims of a swarm of murderous insects, so overwhelmed were they with vessels seeking sanctuary.

As the Tome Keepers' fleet advanced towards the morass, yet more ships poured through the system's Mandeville point behind them, on course for Anakletos. All of them were civilian vessels – gas-cloud harvesters, mining rigs, colony ships, agri-stock transports… There seemed to be no end to the mass of humanity pouring into Anakletos's space. No other worlds in the system were habitable, although some were home to small mining operations working out of habitat domes and crewed by desperate Imperial dregs. The only world that could even remotely hope to cope with the sheer volume of traffic in the system was Anakletos.

The vox-net was filled with the shouts of exhausted ship commanders, the pleas of desperate refugees and the impatient orders of exasperated Ecclesiarchal auxiliary boat captains from hundreds of ships. The crew of every arriving vessel demanded shelter, repair and supply and reported devastation from whence it had come.

'It has been impossible to maintain order,' said Commodore-Captain Phinelus Horagh, commander of the Mercury-class battle cruiser K*harybdis* and leader of the Imperial Navy war group left behind by Task Force XI after it had passed through the Anakletos System en route to Argovon. His voice echoed through the bridge of the *Hariwok*, which was unusually quiet to ensure the commander's words could be heard by all. Only the gentle rumble of the ship's engines, the monotone binharic babbling of the ship's servitors and the pressing of keys and buttons by the crew could be heard. The officers, wearing pressed uniforms the same colour as the Tome Keepers' armour, passed orders through hand signals or via data-slates so as not to disturb their Space Marine masters. To watch them at work was to witness the epitome of martial professionalism.

'*More ships arrive every day,*' the naval commander continued. '*Many are full to the brim with starving and terrified refugees and have little to no supplies. Uprisings from the desperate are not uncommon. We have had to deploy boarding parties to put down rebellions and cancel supply runs to some ships and divert resources to stop others facing full-scale riots. We have sustained casualties and inflicted many. I have troops stationed to keep order on over a dozen civilian vessels. I do not have forces to deploy permanently to many others.*'

'What of the local leadership?' asked Nasiem.

They have no idea what they are dealing with, thought Epistolary Lykandos. He was one of many Tome Keepers on the *Hariwok*'s bridge listening to the commodore-captain brief Captain Nasiem as to the situation on Anakletos. Sephax, Kae, Gadatas, Sanduq and Manishtu were all present. All of the Tome Keepers had expected a degree of turmoil in the system upon their arrival. None had quite anticipated what they'd found.

'*It is clear they are overwhelmed,*' said Horagh. '*They have never seen anything like this. They perhaps welcome some tens of millions of pilgrims across a local year. They have received many more than that in the past few weeks and in a much worse condition. It took Deacon Grantyde Flinnikar – the governor – some time to accept our help. They said the situation was a local matter and none of the business of the Imperial Navy. Other Navy ships that arrived here tell me they received the same communication. There are twenty-two others my war group has been coordinating with, though none are at a full state of capability. Almost all have sustained damage, and most are low on munitions.*'

Three are incapable of moving. They have come from a dozen warzones, all under necron or heretic attack.'

Nasiem was not pleased. It did not take Lykandos's powers of telepathy to determine that fact.

'My war group is also not untouched. Xenos species appear to be fleeing the Nexus. Some came here. I could not identify the species, there might have been more than one. We destroyed their ships – most, I expect, were civilian rather than military. Still, they did damage. Four of my escorts are operating at around eighty-per-cent capability now. It is also important to know that the deacon has seized crusade supply ships for his own population and the refugees. I could not interfere without using lethal force. I determined that, given the volatility of the situation, it was not advisable. That was when I contacted task force command. Things must be getting desperate down there. We need to keep things moving, get the refugees out of the system and start repairing these ships.'

'I understand, Commodore-Captain. We will resolve every matter once we have dealt with the insurrection on the ground. What can you tell us about that?' asked Nasiem.

'Very little, lord. The deacon barely acknowledges that it is happening, at least in discussions with me. My war group has in its holds the Nine Hundred and First Garlen Lightfoot Regiment. I offered to deploy them, with their general's agreement, to aid in protecting strategic locations and to root out the rebels. I was refused. I have fifteen thousand eager soldiers on my ships, Lord, with weapons and no enemy. They would be of great use on the surface, no doubt. Again, the planetary leadership states that this is a local, Ecclesiarchal affair that they can resolve alone. I've heard rumours of what has been going on from other ships' captains. There seem to have been at least seven major incidents so far, with thousands killed and many more injured. The rebels have targeted refugee camps, holy shrines and granaries. The frateris militia are rounding up suspects and carrying out public executions. They appear to have had little positive effect – and quite possibly the opposite to that intended. It is like trying to use a shovel where one needs tweezers.'

+Everything is completely out of control,+ said Lykandos to Nasiem, pressing the words telepathically into the captain's mind. +This action of ours will be a political one as much as military. We will have to tread even more carefully around the Ecclesiarchy than we previously thought.+

Or we shall have to be much firmer, said Nasiem, communicating with Lykandos with his thoughts.

+That also,+ replied Lykandos. +However, we need much more information.+

Agreed, said Nasiem.

If he allowed himself, Lykandos could feel the terror, confusion and anger racing through the souls of everyone aboard the ships in Anakletos's orbit at once. Such a volume of raw emotion would destroy him, had he no psychic guards in place. He could feel it in bursts striking his mental barriers with quick, dull thuds and dissipating

in flares of energy. It was somehow burning hot and freezing cold all at once. In his mind's eye, it sparked in flashes of crimson, amber and azure – amongst countless other hues – against a rippling, translucent shield.

While Lykandos could hold back waves of emotive energy, he could also allow through that which he willed. His eye was drawn to the Hariwok's watch officer. Something had the woman's attention on the central augur system. He could sense the increase in her heart rate and brain activity. Fear spiked in her.

+Speak,+ he instructed. He did not put words into her head, instead merely seeding a psychic prompt that would push her to raise what she had observed.

She approached the command dais upon which all the Tome Keepers stood.

'Lords, I request permission to speak.'

Lykandos could hear a slight wobble of nerves in her voice, but otherwise she was loud and clear.

+Allow it, Nasiem,+ said Lykandos to his captain.

'Granted, Lieutenant,' said Nasiem.

'Anomalous ship movement identified. Civilian vessel on impact course with Siluria-class light cruiser Bright Crusader.'

Lykandos delved into Commodore-Captain Horagh's mind to learn more about the targeted ship. The Bright Crusader had been driven to Anakletos from the Paradyce System by the necrons. Well-captained by Hrenlior Prynlatius, who had insisted that civilians be taken care of before his own ship and crew, it had become a beacon for civilian vessels as it distributed supplies and brought about good order amongst the morass of ships in its vicinity. Its medicae staff and servitors treated the sick and injured, its troops prevented crime, and its drop-ships ensured the efficient movement of resources and people. The Hariwok was too far away for the Tome Keepers to help it.

'Show me,' said Nasiem.

A screen descended from the bridge's ceiling. Shown on it was the read-out from the central augur system. As the Tome Keepers' fleet had drawn closer to Anakletos, the augur had picked up a clearer and clearer picture of the anarchy that was the swarm of voidcraft in the world's orbit. Thousands of green dots flocked over the screen.

It is a disaster, thought Lykandos. To hear it from Commodore-Captain Horagh was one thing, to feel the raw emotion of the people also… But to see so many ships like this was another thing entirely.

The watch officer had highlighted the civilian vessel – identified only by the code 874-ΛΦ-2 – in an ominous red. The Bright Crusader was similarly marked. The course of 874-ΛΦ-2 was plotted, showing a collision was imminent.

'Vessel Eight-Seven-Four-Lambda-Phi-Two is the size of a Tempest-class frigate,' the watch officer said.

That made the ship approximately half the size of the Bright Crusader.

It will be catastrophic.

'It must be the insurrection,' said Sephax. 'It must be destroyed as soon as possible.'

'Most likely,' agreed Nasiem.

'A technical issue?' suggested Kae. 'The question must be raised, however unlikely it seems that it might be the case.'

'Lykandos?' asked Nasiem.

Lykandos tapped into the emotive energy flowing around the two vessels. The impact of the sheer terror, the utterly hopeless desperation and the anguish of thousands on board both ships felt like a power maul strike to the brain. He endured the pain for thirty seconds. It was only made worse by the sense of those aboard 874-ΛΦ-2 who wanted this to happen, who were causing it and relishing the havoc that would ensue once their mission was complete. Their evil desire was like a dagger through his heart.

To know their pain is to fight for them all the harder when the time comes.

Every time Lykandos did this, his soul grew darker. The rings around his eyes grew deeper and he became a little more distant from his battle-brothers. He might have once been a Greyshield, but he had seen and felt more pain, misery and horror than even Nasiem had.

'No technical issue,' he said. 'The malevolent intent behind this is tangible.'

'My thanks, Epistolary,' said Nasiem.

Lykandos thought of Sephax. The Orator was no less experienced in battle than Lykandos was, but he was utterly single-minded in purpose. His only thought would be of vengeance.

'That settles it. We must make planetfall with all haste,' said the Orator.

Lykandos felt a pang in his gut. The same pang he felt whenever he considered Sephax's overly aggressive demeanour. It was anger but also it was envy.

What must it be like, to not only be ignorant of the despair, fear and pain of so many but also of the true horrors that dwell in the minds of men in all the galaxy?

It was a question Lykandos had asked himself many times.

I am blessed and cursed, thought Lykandos to himself. *Blessed with knowledge and a desire to seek more of it… Yet that knowledge and desire condemns me to an alienated life and to feel such… horror.*

'Ahead full speed,' ordered Nasiem. 'Prime weapons. Destroy Eight-Seven-Four-Lambda-Phi-Two the moment it comes into range.'

It was no easy decision to order the deaths of thousands of innocents. But sometimes it had to be done if it meant saving the lives of several thousand more.

Lykandos felt the Hariwok lurch as it accelerated at speed.

'Lord, it is my duty to tell you that Eight-Seven-Four-Lambda-Phi-Two is far enough away that we may not succeed. If we fire too early, another vessel might move into the path of our munitions accidentally,' said Commodore Belessunu.

'I understand, Commodore. However, my orders stand,' said Nasiem.

Several seconds passed in tense silence.

'Vessel Eight-Seven-Four-Lambda-Phi-Two is less than five minutes from its target,' said Belessunu. 'We cannot reach optimal distance from it before then.'

'Push the Hariwok harder.'

Lykandos knew the commodore stopped himself from objecting and just followed the order. They were not going to make it.

Minutes passed.

Nasiem said nothing, but Lykandos could feel his anger. It was taking all the captain's strength to stop him from tearing the bridge apart.

Everyone watched in mournful silence as the red dot labelled 874-ΛΦ-2 overlapped with that labelled Bright Crusader. In a blink both disappeared.

In an instant, the pain and fear and misery of thousands of souls was extinguished. The emotive energy lost all its driving force and hung without movement in Lykandos's mind's eye. Slowly it dissipated, as dust in the air. For the briefest moment, the Epistolary felt a kind of peace, a silence. But then it was gone. It was replaced only with even more agony as those people on the ships struck by the enormous debris chunks resulting from the explosion faced horror and death of their own.

'What is the damage?' asked Nasiem.

'Reports are coming in now, Lord,' said the watch officer.

'I would speak with the deacon in the meantime.'

'Vox chatter has increased twofold in the aftermath of the explosion, Lord,' said the master vox-officer after a few seconds. 'Panic has already spread. The planet is being bombarded with demands. Those ship captains who don't want to put their passengers on the ground now are demanding supplies with even more fervour than before. They're afraid of facing revolt if they do not receive aid.'

Though many ships' vox-links were protected against those who would listen to the words exchanged, Space Marine vessels possessed data-spirits that had little trouble intercepting transmissions from Imperial civilian craft.

'Find a way to cut through it all.'

'Yes, Lord.'

'Lord, I have the damage reports,' stated the watch officer.

'I will hear them now, Lieutenant.'

'Nothing is left of *Eight-Seven-Four-Lambda-Phi-Two* or the *Bright Crusader*. A dozen nearby vessels were destroyed. Thirty-nine more ships in the broader vicinity report serious damage and dozens more report being struck by debris. Loss of life incalculable – we have no record of passenger listings, and most of the ships will not have had such information in any case. Likely to be in the hundreds of thousands at the least.'

There was no telling how far the rot went. Any one of the ships surrounding them could belong to the insurrection, waiting to capitalise.

How many more ships do they control? wondered Lykandos.

'I need to speak with the deacon. Now!' said Nasiem.

'It cannot be done, Lord,' replied the master vox-officer. 'The channels are flooded.'

'Then I shall send a message to every ship here. Mark as priority alpha-vermilion. Let them be in no doubt that the Adeptus Astartes are here and have words for them. It is time we made our presence felt.'

'Silence on the bridge for the captain,' barked Company Champion Manishtu.

'The vox is yours, Lord,' said the master vox-officer.

Silence fell. Nasiem stepped forward on the command dais.

'This is Captain Nasiem bal Tergu, captain of the Adeptus Astartes Tome Keepers Third Company and Keeper of the Key, speaking from the strike cruiser *Hariwok*. We are here to destroy the insurrection and thus restore order. We know you are afraid. We know you have been through terrible hardship. But we expect you to act with the control and decency all citizens of the Imperium should display. I ask for your patience. I ask for calm. Aid has arrived. The Emperor protects. End message.'

Lykandos would have smiled, had he still had the ability to do such a thing after everything he had endured and seen.

He uses the power of the Adeptus Astartes to assert his authority and uses empathy to win respect and cooperation without threats of force and violence. He does not demand anything from them, for he knows they will do what he needs them to regardless. He is a true leader.

'Vox chatter is already dying down substantially,' said the master vox-officer.

'Ship movements much reduced,' said the watch officer.

'Good,' said Nasiem. 'Now I will speak with the deacon. Lykandos, Kae, Sephax – with me. I shall speak with him in the private counsel chamber.'

The counsel chamber was situated close to the bridge. It only had capacity for a small number of fully armoured Space Marines to sit at the round table at its centre, which had been carved from a single block of Istrouman pyroxenite. The walls were sparsely decorated. In this room, the voice of each warrior was equal. Upon the centre of the table was a hololithic projector; emanating from it came a flickering image of Deacon Grantyde Flinnikar in electric-blue light. Even in this poorly defined projection, Lykandos could see that the deacon was visibly exhausted and agitated.

'Deacon Flinnikar,' said Captain Nasiem. 'As stated in my prior message, we are here to resolve the insurrection issue. Anakletos needs to be made safe to ensure the continued processing of refugees and the continued supply of Indomitus Crusade forces in the Argovon System. Though as a captain of the Adeptus Astartes, I am neither required to ask permission nor to give notice of the deployment of my warriors to your world, I am choosing to notify you now out of respect for your title and the Ministorum. I will deploy the bulk of my strength. I am aware that you refused the aid of the Nine Hundred and First Garlen Lightfoot. They would have been able to provide you with improved security in a number of important locations. You *will* permit them now. The incident that has just occurred in orbit has demonstrated that the situation on your world is out of hand.'

Lykandos pried into the deacon's mind for insights. The man was just about keeping his head while conversing with Nasiem.

'*We have no way of knowing if the collision was a mere accident,*' said Flinnikar.

We do, thought Lykandos, *but they would not reveal the means by which they did to the deacon. The man would have little understanding or care for telepathic powers, and if he thought the Tome Keepers were using them, he'd be, at best, uncooperative and, at worst, accuse them of witchcraft.*

Neither of which are conducive to the successful eradication of a burgeoning insurrection.

'Regardless, it shows how dangerous the orbital situation is and the importance of restoring order,' said Nasiem. 'What say you of the Astra Militarum?'

'I *have complete confidence in the frateris militia, Captain. I'm sure, combined with your warriors, that will be more than sufficient.*'

Why this resistance? thought Lykandos.

He looked into the deacon's eyes. He saw fear. He saw shame. He saw inexperience.

+He presents himself as strong, only to make himself appear weaker than he would have otherwise,+ Lykandos said to Nasiem.

Where is his honesty? Where is his self-awareness?

'Deacon, given that the security of this world directly affects one of the Imperium's crusade fleets, commissioned by the Avenging Son himself, it is a matter of principle that its forces play a role in the task, regardless of your belief in their necessity. You will grant them permission to deploy.'

We will have greater influence over what they do, how and when, thought Lykandos of the Astra Militarum. The Tome Keepers would need reliable allies on Anakletos. The deacon was unlikely to be one of them.

Do it, priest, thought Lykandos. *Allow them.*

'The crusade will certainly look favourably upon those who commit to its righteous cause to smite xenos and heretical foes, wherever they are found, and liberate the Emperor's people,' continued Nasiem.

Lykandos felt the priest's whole demeanour change at the mention of favour. His ambition was at the forefront, his eagerness for plaudits to be piled upon him.

'Agreed,' said Flinnikar. '*The Astra Militarum will be welcomed, their commander will be given relevant intelligence clearances, and we will advise as to where their forces are best placed to aid the situation.*'

'We will meet with you on the surface to discuss the insurrection,' said Nasiem.

'*It will be as you say, Captain,*' said the deacon. '*I will arrange a special sitting of the council.*'

'Very well, Deacon. Nasiem out.'

The captain pressed an icon built into the table. The projection blinked off. The Tome Keepers were now bathed in the warm, flickering light of braziers rather than the cold blue of the hololith.

'Your thoughts, Lykandos?' asked Nasiem. 'He was reluctant, even when speaking with a Space Marine captain. Should we be suspicious?'

'I did not sense treachery in him, Nasiem,' said Lykandos. 'Merely the weakness and ambition of a man overwhelmed by his circumstances. I would not be surprised if the state of affairs on the surface is much more severe than we have had reason to believe thus far. The governor and his people will also be unpredictable allies. They will be afraid, potentially dangerous.'

'I agree,' said Kae. 'We should be prepared for anything, including a total population uprising.'

'I do not like handling men like him gently,' said Sephax.

'You and I both, brother,' said Nasiem. 'But his willing cooperation will be of much greater use to us than him using the power of the Ecclesiarchy to hinder our actions out of pettiness.'

'I did not sense anything that suggested he knew of our Chapter,' said Lykandos. 'If he is unaware of our unfortunate history with his organisation and it stays that way, our mission here will be made much easier.'

'We shall see,' said Sephax. 'But we must be ready to stamp our full authority on this place. Ecclesiarchy or not, our mission comes first.'

'There will be violence enough to sate you, Sephax, regardless. I have no doubt of that,' said Lykandos with obvious distaste.

'Do not accuse me of bloodthirst, Librarian. I am a Tome Keeper. I understand pragmatism as well as any warrior who bears the Tome Celestial on their pouldron. I do not crave unnecessary conflict with those we should be allies with. But politics should not win out.'

'And it shall not, Sephax,' said Nasiem. 'It is likely the Ecclesiarchy will frustrate us all, as it has many of our predecessors before us. Study the events of the Sanctimonia Conflict, the Nova Terra Interregnum, the Laanath Rifts and the Sublimium Conflagration. They will teach us much.'

'Aye, Captain,' the Tome Keepers said in unison.

'We will all join the deacon's council. Kae, see to it that our warriors are ready and the ships aid in the orbital crisis as much as they are able. Three squads will stay in orbit, under Techmarine Rabash's command. The rest of the battle-brothers will join us on the surface.'

Deacon Flinnikar's palace-basilica was built atop the Plateau of Saint Hyrenthia Thrice-Martyred, overlooking the shrine city of Tiryns. A glorious display of Ecclesiarchal power, it was constructed of polished white marble, with psalms, prayers and words of praise to the Emperor inlaid on its flanks with gold. Enormous royal-purple banners fluttered brilliantly in the wind above it, hung between columns a hundred and sixty feet tall, each one woven with golden thread that proclaimed the greatness of the Imperium and the God-Emperor.

But the palace-basilica's architecture had not just been constructed with aesthetic qualities in mind. Lykandos had seen the anti-air gun positions artfully concealed by statuary of angels and cherubim. Frateris militia wearing grand, boldly coloured uniforms and bearing artisan-crafted lasrifles adorned with silver filigree patrolled battlements decorated with the carved faces of saints.

Lykandos and the other Tome Keepers had been guided through a labyrinth of lavish corridors, lined with the sarcophagi of long-dead Ecclesiarchal dignitaries and lit brightly by the local sun's rays. The light poured through enormous stained-glass windows, each four times his height and twice his width. Their images told the stories of martyred saints and glorious Imperial victories; one depicted the Emperor sat atop the Golden Throne, adored by his subjects.

Despite all this grandeur, Lykandos saw that the interior had also been cunningly designed for military defence. The faint flicker of refractor fields protected the windows. What appeared to be heavy, wooden doors were in fact solid metal, with an expensive veneer. Different corridors and chambers served as choke points and rallying points and were laid out in such a manner that any attacker would easily get disorientated.

As the Tome Keepers strode through, accompanied by the deacon's private secretary and her servants, they passed groups of monks, acolytes, priests and nuns. All wore fine robes of azure, crimson, amber, jet and cream, and stopped to bow deeply when they encountered the Space Marines.

They all appear to be calm, Nasiem had thought to Lykandos.

It was all a lie.

+Do not trust what you see, Captain,+ Lykandos had said. +Many of them feel great fear. And its primary cause is not the presence of Adeptus Astartes warriors.+

Now they were in the council chamber itself. It was no less grand than anything else they had seen in the palace-basilica. The ceiling reached a thousand feet into the air and was topped by a huge dome. Every panel wall had been painted over beautifully with yet more images of the radiant God-Emperor and his loving, worshipping subjects.

Blind faith, celebrated over everything else.

There were other images in this chamber, of the Emperor smiting his foes by his mere presence. His enemies burned horribly in his light, their faces contorted by agony, screaming as flames licked their blood-red fur. Their wide mouths revealed sets of wicked-looking fangs. They had horned tails, patches of scaly skin, chiropteran wings and webbed feet. Somehow, the artists had painted into their subjects' expressions a greater pain than the

physical one they were enduring. Lykandos saw regret, even repentance in their eyes. Such was the Emperor's holy power, even the most foul of monsters could not help but be in total awe of it in the end.

Truly masterful, thought Lykandos of the work. *Its beauty makes the blind faith that led to its creation all the more tragic.*

Around the edge of the circular chamber sat Deacon Flinnikar and the twenty-four subdeacons of the council. Each represented one of Anakletos' dioceses, and their marble thrones were decorated according to the saint their region was named for. The throne for the Diocese of Saint Alekin the Drowned had nets, crustaceans and pescids carved into its flanks. The throne for the Diocese of Saint Leagah the Prayer was painted with images of devout acolytes and citizens on their knees, heads bowed and hands together. A banner hung above each throne, the name of its patron saint emblazoned on the fabric in bold writing. The men and women sat on plush purple cushions as the session began.

All this power, wealth and grandiosity, yet they are just weak and terrified people wholly incapable of dealing with the situation they face.

Lykandos read the fear in the chamber. All were afraid of the Space Marines, who stood in the centre of the council hall. They carried no weapons and had mag-locked their helmets to their thigh armour.

It had been Lykandos's idea that they go to the council meeting unarmed. The leadership of Anakletos would be more likely to comply if the Adeptus Astartes voluntarily appeared less threatening. Lykandos wanted them to have no reason to cause any more problems for the Tome Keepers than they almost certainly would regardless.

Nasiem, Kae, Lykandos and Sephax had been welcomed with full honours and fanfare. It had taken them all by surprise. The Ecclesiarchy was supposed to harbour little liking for the Tome Keepers. Lykandos had scanned all their minds. There was no hatred there. These people did not know of their organisation's history with the Chapter.

'Deacon-governor, honoured subdeacons,' said Nasiem. 'You know why my brothers and I are here. Our goal is nothing less than the total annihilation of the insurrection you face and the restoration of peace and order to your world.'

'Welcome, Captain Nasiem of the Adeptus Astartes Tome Keepers, to Anakletos. We will do all we can to aid you in your honourable quest.'

The deacon did not raise his voice in the slightest, but the chamber's acoustics carried his words throughout the entire space.

+I do not need to be a telepath in this place, Captain,+ said Lykandos psychically to Nasiem. +His heart beats so strongly. We are only here because he felt he had no option. He is reluctant.+

All we need is his cooperation, thought Nasiem. *Willing or otherwise, it matters not.*

'Welcome,' the subdeacons said in unison. Many nodded and showed empty palms.

Nasiem nodded.

'You all have the thanks of my brothers and I,' he said. 'If we are to resolve this quickly, as we all surely wish to do, I require you to provide us with all intelligence you have acquired about the rebellion. Every scrap of data is relevant and vital, I ask you to spare nothing.'

'We will provide everything you require, Captain Nasiem,' said Flinnikar.

'Thank you, Deacon-governor. Please tell us, how did this begin? How many attacks have there been? What is the name of the group responsible? The recent catastrophe in orbit has shown that the situation is serious indeed.'

'As I said earlier, we cannot know if that was not simple technical failures – so many ships in orbit are experiencing them – or even the Stilling.'

How ignorant is this man? thought Lykandos.

'The Stilling would have the opposite effect,' said Sephax.

'We know it was an intentional attack,' said Lykandos. 'We studied their trajectory and speed. It was too precise for anything else,' he lied.

'My brother speaks the truth, Deacon Flinnikar,' said Nasiem. 'Continue; my other questions.'

Lykandos did not pay full attention to the rest of the answers given by the deacon and subdeacons, taking care to hear enough only to compare what they said with their thoughts. Nasiem, Kae and Sephax were more than capable of memorising and assessing every detail of what they were told. It was the Epistolary's role to listen beyond the speech. To hear the truths no amount of smiles, confident gestures and rehearsed oratory could conceal.

The councillors rattled on for several minutes, blissfully unaware that Lykandos was probing their minds for what they didn't say. The Epistolary learned much about humanity that he never intended to uncover when delving into minds to seek out specific information. Even in situations such as these, where before them stood four Space Marines, they could not focus on the task at hand. They flitted, almost at random, from subject to subject, person to person. Several were thinking of the concubines they were hoping to soon see. Some were concerned others were aware that they were evading their personal tithes. Many were plotting how they would use this opportunity to bring about the demise of one or many of their colleagues. Others were concerned for the plight of the refugees in their respective districts. It was clear that many feared for the availability of supplies. They thought of a million and one things, these men and women.

But Lykandos knew how to see the pattern, how to pick through and find the thoughts that mattered.

There's no way he can get away with this, thought one.

There's been twice that many attacks in my district alone, thought a second.

Please let them believe it, thought another.

That was all Lykandos needed to hear.

+We are being deliberately misled,+ he said directly into Nasiem's mind.

No sooner had he sent this than one of the chamber's immense doors opened. A bald man wearing the plain white robes of an acolyte walked through hastily, taking pains to avoid looking at the Space Marines as he made his way directly to Deacon Flinnikar. The sound of his steps reverberated around the chamber as silence fell amongst the Space Marines and the councillors. All stared at him. Lykandos saw the man was carrying a note in his hand.

Lykandos pierced the man's mind. The acolyte was completely ignorant of what the message contained. Such knowledge was clearly beneath his station.

Deacon Flinnikar took the note from the acolyte's outstretched hands and read it. Every so often, his eyes lifted from the page and to the Space Marines. His mouth moved silently as he read. When he had finished, he folded the paper carefully and dismissed the acolyte. He kept the note.

'Ah, so you are the Tome Keepers. I had my acolytes study our reference libraries for your name, and they found you. The Ministorum remembers you from the events at Sanctimonia millennia ago and, more recently, at the Laanath Rifts. And now, as we attempt to manage an ongoing crisis, you once again disrupt the Emperor's work by distracting his servants with this meeting and your endless questions.'

'A crisis you have allowed to get out of your control, and questions you have failed to adequately answer,' said Sephax tersely.

Fool, thought Lykandos. *We do not need to make this worse.* Still, he had to admit, the Orator was not incorrect in his pronouncement – and perhaps it was too late to salvage what they could from this.

'"The Chapter demonstrated unorthodox attitudes in the extreme," one of my ancient predecessors writes, according to my acolytes' diligent research,' said Flinnikar with barely concealed disdain.

Lykandos sensed the deacon's growing sense of triumph.

'"Desecrators of a tomb of martyrs," another records. The

Cardinal Palatine of Sanctimonia, over four thousand years ago, accused the Tome Keepers of "dereliction of duty." For shame!'

'For shame,' echoed several of the subdeacons.

Though not all, Lykandos noted.

+Nasiem, they do not all share the deacon's indignation,+ he said.

'Deacon Flinnikar,' Nasiem said firmly, 'if the best evidence against my brotherhood is a handful of anecdotal accounts from four thousand years ago, then I believe you have little cause for concern. The evidence of our willingness to cooperate with you and aid you in the handling of this crisis has been clear for all here to see.' The captain opened his arms wide. 'We have engaged in the meetings you have arranged without complaint. We are here speaking when, by the rights of the Indomitus Crusade, we could have demanded your compliance. My ships seek to bring about order in orbit as we speak. I understand you did not choose this situation, that it has been thrust upon you and that you lack the resources to deal with the myriad challenges that have arisen. We can be a great ally to you here.'

Lykandos saw many of the subdeacons staring at Flinnikar now. He did not have to delve into their thoughts to know that Nasiem had already swayed many of them – more than those who had harboured misgivings over the deacon's methods minutes before.

'Whether you care for the Tome Keepers or not,' continued Nasiem, 'this matter is not merely a local one. The events on Anakletos are Indomitus Crusade business and concern the success of Task Force Eleven of Battle Group Kallides of Fleet Primus. One way or another, eventually forces would have been sent here to ensure supplies being transported through your space continued to move unimpeded to the ongoing campaign in the Argovon System. If the war effort there was in any way hindered by a failure on the part of Anakletos's leadership, Fleet Primus command would hold those responsible to account without hesitation. And they would have the backing of not only Groupmaster Marran of Battle Group Kallides but also the Avenging Son, Primarch Roboute Guilliman, himself.'

The thought of Imperial justice coming their way was enough to inspire terror in all of the Ecclesiarchal leaders in the room, including the recalcitrant deacon.

'Is that a threat, Captain?' he asked, his voice noticeably weaker than before.

'Merely a statement of fact, Deacon,' said Nasiem.

Just tell him, Flinnikar, Lykandos heard one of the subdeacons think.

Just pretend you forgot the other information, thought another.

Do not bend to their threats, hold firm, you have them, thought a third.

+Nasiem, they are still withholding information.+

Understood.

'I would be most grateful if you could continue with answering our questions. I am sure there is much more you could tell us,' Nasiem prompted.

One of the subdeacons whose mind Lykandos was yet to read spoke. She was younger than many of the others, though the Epistolary could tell from a cursory glance of her faculties that she possessed considerably more nous than many in the chamber.

'Deacon Flinnikar, if you would be so kind as to allow me to contribute?'

'Yes, of course, Subdeacon Jengellahr,' said the deacon, evidently surprised that a member of the council had spoken, yet clearly relieved that the immediate pressure was being taken off him.

Subdeacon Jengellahr nodded her thanks.

'Thank you for sharing the information you have collected about the Tome Keepers and the insurrectionist threat, Deacon Flinnikar. You presented a truly superb précis of our confirmed intelligence. Might I humbly suggest that your grace share with the Tome Keepers our less well-attested information? Some of our theories, some of the rumours we have collected, that you clearly believed – in all sincerity – would waste the Adeptus Astartes' precious time?'

Clever. She gives the deacon a way to comply with our requests and yet still save face in front of the council.

'Sage advice indeed, Subdeacon Jengellahr,' said Flinnikar. 'Captain Nasiem, I will have all our notes and, indeed, most tenuous theories, collated and provided for you at the earliest opportunity. I apologise if it felt at all as if I had not given you enough information – I merely wanted to present to you only the facts, not waste your time with unsubstantiated details, many of which, I should say, are contradictory. Whilst I must stress that this is currently not fully based on checked intelligence, some theories contest there are multiple insurrections, which could mean the total number of heretics is some three times the total I informed you of earlier. There have been a number of events – building collapses and the like – which I am sure have been merely accidents, yet some have attributed them to the enemy here. Again, I cannot confirm that these were indeed intended attacks, but if somehow they were, it means that there could have been up to four times as many successful heretic assaults on Anakletos. Almost certainly nonsense, but now you are aware.'

Filthy liar, thought Lykandos. *Concealing all that from us?*

Lykandos saw Sephax tense at this new information. The Orator clearly saw things in the same light as he did.

+Say nothing, Orator, we have our intelligence. I share your frustration, but now is not the time to voice it.+

Sephax said nothing, either to the deacon or in response to Lykandos. The Epistolary noticed the grip of Sephax's armoured gauntlet tightening.

'Thank you for your cooperation, Deacon,' said Nasiem. 'We shall be about our business and see that this rebellion is crushed, as it deserves.'

The vessel's interior was as unremarkable as its outer hull. Gunmetal instruments with blinking red, blue and amber lights and muted green panels sat on gunmetal decking, their machine-spirits making the contented beeps and chirps of constructs performing the routine processes they were designed to, without hindrance or difficulty. The ship appeared to have been completed in the most recent of years, fresh from Imperial foundries. But it was missing small but vital elements of craft designed and produced by the Adeptus Mechanicus for use by the Navis Imperialis. Along miles of halls, corridors and chambers there was not even the smallest image honouring the Emperor. Not one candle burned in his name. There was no hint of the scent of burning incense from religious rituals, just the tang of counterseptic disinfectants and bare metal. The endless thrumming of the ship's engines was not drowned out by an internal vox-system alive with the reading of psalms or hymnals whilst not in use by the crew for military purposes. The thousands of mortal crew who went about their duties with the utmost professionalism wore plain grey fatigues, freshly pressed and starched, speaking only when they had orders to issue or reports to make. None made the sign of the aquila when addressing a comrade, carried personal prayer books or mentioned the Emperor's name.

On the ship's bridge, two power armour-clad warriors were engaged in conversation.

'So this is Anakletos,' said one, the leader. 'Tell me about it, Thirteen.'

'Ministorum-run shrine world. For millennia it has been a moderately attractive location for pilgrims. Otherwise it has been remarkable only for its lack of remarkability. Leadership has been mediocre at best for centuries, bar one or two exceptions. Even their achievements were merely to restore a handful of crumbling cathedrals.'

'Its fortunes have evidently changed.'

'Indeed. It is the only Imperial-controlled world for light years which has not been affected by what the Imperium calls 'the Stilling', the malaise that for a time affected our own crew. As a result, it is now directly on the exit route for those fleeing the warp-silencing veil that the necrons established in the Nephilim Sector and directly on the entry route for supply ships and troop transports heading for the Argovon System. Both have put much pressure on the world's resources. Rebellions have sprung up. There have been many attacks. The planet's leadership has so far failed to contain any of it. The situation is ideal for development. The world is on the cusp of anarchy. And the Tome Keepers have sailed into the heart of it.'

'Very good indeed. The embers are ripe for stoking. All of the mortals will go to the surface. We have an uprising to foment. All but a handful of the warriors will also deploy with us. Be careful with who stays, Thirteen. I will have no one attempt to leave with my ship.'

'I will leave Nineteen in command and Twelve as enforcer.'

'An effective combination. I approve.'

'Your orders, for the surface?'

'Use your imagination to start with, Thirteen. Give the mortals autonomy, don't give the Tome Keepers reason to expect order of any kind. Make sure you equip the locals appropriately as well. We will bleed them deeply.'

HEIRS OF REASON CONTINUES WITH PART III IN THE NEXT ISSUE OF WHITE DWARF.

INSIDE THE STUDIO

As we come to the end of the magazine, we take a look at the games the studio staff have been playing and the models they've been painting. This month, we've got vampires, ghosts, heroes, beasts, something Risky and a couple of Space Marines to keep an eye on things.

C ampaigns! That's the word on everybody's lips in the Warhammer Studio right now. Well, that and 'hello', as we all gather for the first time in a year and a half.

Of course, military campaigns need armies, so everyone has been busy building and painting new models in preparation for the many different studio campaigns that will be taking place over the next few months. Here in the *White Dwarf* team, most of us have been busy painting models for Warhammer Age of Sigmar, which conveniently also count towards our Hobby Bingo challenge for 2022. We've also been playing a bit of Risk: Warhammer 40,000, which has just been released here in the UK. You can read more about it below and see our latest projects over the next few pages.

RISK: WARHAMMER 40,000

Having returned to the studio, Lyle, Andrew, Matt and Jonathan cracked open the copy of Risk: Warhammer 40,000 we'd been lucky enough to get our hands on. With the game set on Vigilus, Matt consolidated his Aeldari forces around the Oteck Hivesprawl, containing Andrew's strung-out Chaos Space Marines in the Ork Scrap Cities. Lyle, the only person to have played Risk before (yes, really!), used Marneus Calgar (+1 to the highest dice) and his Ultramarines to defeat Abaddon (reroll 1s) and quickly claim 'Australia'. Check your local gaming store for Risk: Warhammer 40,000.

CHAPLAIN BY CALUM MCPHERSON

Calum: My Chaplain is called Orton Tancrede, and he's heavily inspired by Aaron Dembski-Bowden's *Helsreach* novel. I sprayed him Chaos Black and then applied a zenithal spray of Mechanicus Standard Grey. Once this was dry, I applied thinned-down Black Templar to bring back the colour and added battle damage with Leadbelcher to show he's been fighting hard.

SPACE WOLVES INTERCESSOR BY TOM MOORE

Tom: I painted this display model using the 'Eavy Metal colour scheme for the Space Wolves. I used a Russ Grey basecoat followed by a soft shade created by mixing Rhinox Hide and The Fang and then a deeper shade of pure Rhinox Hide. This was followed by a highlight of Fenrisian Grey and a finer one of Blue Horror. Finally, for the dots on the sharp edges I used Blue horror mixed with White Scar.

HOBBY BINGO

A1 10 pts	B1 10 pts	C1 10 pts	D1 10 pts	E1 10 pts
HERO OR CHARACTER	**FORTIFICATION OR SCENERY**	**HERO OR CHARACTER**	**KITBASHED MODEL**	**LORD OF WAR OR BEHEMOTH**
Expert Level: Warhammer 40,000	Expert Level: Warhammer Age of Sigmar	Expert Level: Warhammer Age of Sigmar	Expert Level: Warhammer Age of Sigmar	Expert Level: Warhammer Age of Sigmar
A2 10 pts	**B2** 10 pts	**C2** 10 pts	**D2** 10 pts	**E2** 10 pts
UNIT OF 5+ MODELS	**UNIT OF 2+ MODELS**	**VEHICLE OR MONSTER**	**UNIT OF 2+ MODELS**	**UNIT OF 10+ MODELS**
Expert Level: Any System	Expert Level: Warhammer Age of Sigmar	Expert Level: Warhammer 40,000	Expert Level: Warhammer Underworlds	Expert Level: Warhammer 40,000
A3 10 pts	**B3** 10 pts	**C3** 10 pts	**D3** 10 pts	**E3** 10 pts
UNIT OF 10+ MODELS	**KITBASHED MODEL**	**ANY MODEL**	**VEHICLE OR MONSTER**	**FORTIFICATION OR SCENERY**
Expert Level: Warhammer Age of Sigmar	Expert Level: Warhammer 40,000	Expert Level: Any System	Expert Level: Warhammer Age of Sigmar	Expert Level: Warhammer Age of Sigmar
A4 10 pts	**B4** 10 pts	**C4** 10 pts	**D4** 10 pts	**E4** 10 pts
UNIT OF 2+ MODELS	**VEHICLE OR MONSTER**	**UNIT OF 5+ MODELS**	**UNIT OF 10+ MODELS**	**HERO OR CHARACTER**
Expert Level: Warhammer 40,000	Expert Level: Warhammer Age of Sigmar	Expert Level: Kill Team	Expert Level: Warhammer 40,000	Expert Level: Warhammer 40,000
A5 10 pts	**B5** 10 pts	**C5** 10 pts	**D5** 10 pts	**E5** 10 pts
LORD OF WAR OR BEHEMOTH	**UNIT OF 10+ MODELS**	**HERO OR CHARACTER**	**UNIT OF 5+ MODELS**	**VEHICLE OR MONSTER**
Expert Level: Warhammer 40,000	Expert Level: Warhammer Age of Sigmar	Expert Level: Warhammer Age of Sigmar	Expert Level: Warcry	Expert Level: Warhammer 40,000

IN BRIEF

SCORING TABLE
Box: 10
Line: 50
Entire grid: 150

JONATHAN STAPLETON — 10 PTS
Jonathan: After a year working on Necrons, I'm taking a bit of a painting break. I'm thinking about new colour schemes for Astra Militarum, though.

SOPHIE BOSTOCK — 20 PTS
Sophie: I've just finished a kitbashed Vampire Lord and some Dire Wolves and started work on some Adeptus Custodes models that were in my pile of shame!

BEN HUMBER — 20 PTS
Ben: When my fiancée saw my hobby efforts last year, she commented that 'you need to do better, this is embarrassing'. Suitably shamed, I painted a Sentinel.

ANDREW 'YOUR GRACE' KING — 20 PTS
Andrew: I'm continuing with Dominion. By the end of the month, I should have ticked off another box for the Man-skewer Boltboyz. I've also started the Gutrippaz.

DAN HARDEN — 40 PTS
Dan: After many months of them sitting forlornly on my desk, I've finally painted ten Brimstone Horrors to go with the Blue Horrors I painted last year. I painted them green rather than yellow to match the 'magic' colour used on my Disciples of Tzeentch. The Basecoat is Moot Green with a wash of Incubi Darkness and highlights of Moot Green and White Scar.

A4 10 pts
UNIT OF 2+ MODELS
Expert Level: Warhammer 40,000

LYLE LOWERY — 20 PTS
Lyle: I've painted a Dreadblade Harrow for my Nighthaunt this month. I primed the model Chaos Black, then airbrushed grey and white onto the parts I wanted to fade into mist. To bring back the sharp transition between the layers of material, I went back in with a brush and repainted the recesses between them with Abaddon Black.

C5 10 pts
HERO OR CHARACTER
Expert Level: Warhammer Age of Sigmar

MATTHEW HUTSON — 60 PTS
Matt: I've finished another Stormcast Eternal – the Knight-Vexillor! I painted him the same way as last month's models and found Apothecary White especially useful when painting his massive banner. For the bases, I used Astrogranite for the texture and cotton wool sprayed black to create a mist, which shows these warriors are from Ulgu. Next on the list are the Praetors!

C1 10 pts
HERO OR CHARACTER
Expert Level: Warhammer Age of Sigmar

HOBBY BINGO SPOTLIGHT

Each month we'll shine a spotlight on someone's Hobby Bingo achievements. This month, German translator Dirk Wehner has been raising the dead!

Dirk: I wanted my Blood Knights to look terrifying and resplendent in sharp contrast to the shabby Deadwalkers I painted recently. I have a Legion of Blood after all, so they've got to look the part! Vincent from our French translation team has an awesome Slambo that he painted in burnished copper, so I asked him how he did it and used the recipe for my vampires. The basecoat is Screaming Bell, followed by a layer of Fulgurite Copper and some generous shading with Carroburg Crimson. Then the armour is drybrushed with Fulgurite Copper again, followed by a red glaze to bring it all together. Lastly, I applied edge highlights with Runefang Steel. I painted some Dire Wolves after the Blood Knights – a far more relaxing project!